It Is Good That I Was Afflicted

Michael A Palmer, Sr.

IT IS GOOD THAT I WAS AFFLICTED

ISBN: 978-0692665886

Cover Design by Starms Communications, LLC
Photo (back cover) by Pinex Video & Photo
Contributing Author & Editor: Tracy A Palmer

TABLE OF CONTENTS

FORWARD

I first met Michael Palmer around August 21, 2013. At that time he had undergone treatment for a condition known as Necrotizing Fasciitis, which is a severe, potentially-lethal infection of the soft tissues. He had been admitted to the hospital, had undergone debridement of all devitalized tissue, and required time in the intensive care unit. He survived initial treatment for his infection and was subsequently referred to me to begin the process of wound reconstruction. Due to the magnitude of these types of soft tissue defects, we often describe the residual wounds of Necrotizing Fasciitis as "shark bites." Therefore, as a plastic surgeon, I was consulted to address his shark bite. My first impression of Mr. Palmer was that in spite of obvious excruciating pain, he was very cordial and very optimistic. The treatment began with a process called the V.A.C. This procedure is performed in an effort to prepare an open wound for skin grafting. The dressing changes are quite painful and require great strength and fortitude to endure. In spite of this, Mr. Palmer was very compliant and never complained of anything. We went to the operating room on December 18, 2013, where we skin grafted his open wounds and placed the V.A.C. His postoperative course was remarkable for the following. The skin graft "take" was approximately 50%; however, we continued our course and Mr. Palmer healed quicker than any of us could have imagined. He contributed some of his rapid healing to the process of "juicing" which he had clarified for me as a technique to turn fruits and vegetables into a healthy drink.

Throughout my interaction with Mr. Palmer, I found him to be an inspiring, humble and congenial human being. I am happy to have crossed paths with such a determined and affable young man. I am pleased that whatever abilities that I may possess assisted him in his recovery and helped him resume his productive life. I wholeheartedly recommend this book for anyone who is going through or has been through a harrowing, life-changing event. The story of persistence and positive thinking rings through no matter what the circumstances.

Dion Chavis,MD, FACS

Plastic and Reconstructive Surgery Certified; American Board of Plastic Surgery

WORDS OF REFLECTION

It's been almost 18 years since I met Michael Palmer. I can remember passing classes at Ivy Tech and would see him in the hallway. He was a nicely dressed young man in a suit which set him apart from the other students. But on the flip side, I knew he had to be connected with our Heavenly Father because he had such a calm and gentle spirit about him. I officially met Michael when he came into Value City Department Store, where I was working at the time, to put items in layaway. We talked at the front of the store as he was checking out. I found out that he was a believer and belonged to a COGIC church at the time. Throughout the years, Michael has become one of my good friends. He was a counselor, confidant, and friend throughout the years as I was raising my children and navigating through different relationships trying to get it right. I even remember when he married his wife, Tracy.

It was in January 2013 when I met my soulmate. It was always a discussion and promise that Michael would be a part of my wedding by playing musical selections. In July, I gave him a list of the songs that I wanted played for the wedding of my husband, Ronald and myself. I notified Michael the week of July 22nd to see if he had mastered the songs (a joke because he is a master musician) and if he had any issues or concerns. At that time, Michael was complaining of some minor pains but that he would get better and would be on point by the time of the wedding on August 3rd.

It was now the week of the wedding and we are at the first rehearsal on Monday July 29th. Michael and I talked prior to rehearsal and he had complained of some pain but once again, he would be alright by the time of the wedding. After all, we ONLY talked about him playing in my wedding for years. For years he listened to me cry, struggle being a single mother of two, keeping busy in the church, going to school, and working two full time jobs. Friday was the next rehearsal day and everyone was there EXCEPT for Michael. We didn't talk earlier but I knew he would be there and was probably working late since he was working three jobs; two Real Estate ventures and his finance company with his wife, and he was going to school at the time.

We decided to go ahead and start the rehearsal and the singers would sing acapella until Michael got there. I called and texted Michael several times with no response or return phone call; that was not like Michael! Almost 45 minutes into the rehearsal, I received a phone call from Tracy, Michael's wife, reporting that they were on the way to transporting Michael to the hospital for emergency surgery and that he would not be able to play for my wedding. EVERYTHING STOPPED!!! I stopped the rehearsal and told everyone what Tracy had reported in regards to Michaels absence. I began to cry because of the thought of losing another dear friend first and foremost. Secondly, he would not be a part of my special day. The wedding was special because of who I married (Ronald M. Johnson) but was not the same during one part of the wedding because of the song I wanted played for my husband; I decided to have a track played instead. If Michael wasn't going to play the song, then I didn't want it done.

Once Ronald and I returned from our honeymoon, we agreed that I would go see Michael at the hospital. I called Tracy to see if it was okay to visit; she said yes. No one could ever prepare me to see what I saw when I came to his room. I heard reports and other people's opinions on Facebook where Michael's condition and state of being was concerned. I saw tubes, machines, monitors, and nurses coming in and out of the room. As I went to get a hospital gown to put on, I began to break down in tears. Michael's mother and father were in the room. His mother came to console me and I told them it was my wedding he was to be at that Saturday he was rushed to the hospital. His father left out of the room and his mother and I began to talk. About 20 -30 minutes later, we went to Michael's bedside and talked to him. His mother told Michael, "Kim is here to see you." Michael opened his eyes and turned his head and looked at me. The look he had on his face was disappointment and he just stared at me. I made a joke to him that he stood me up on my wedding day and that I would never forgive him. He closed his eyes again; guessing the medicine and drugs he was on had Michael coming in and out. Ronald and I came about three weeks later and Michael was doing much better. Michael was sitting up and reading his Bible when we arrived. I began to cry again because I remember what he looked like just weeks earlier. Ronald and Michael began to talk. Before we left, Ronald prayed for continued healing and to restore him physically, mentally, and that God would get the glory out of this "broken to be made whole" vessel.

So for me, Michael Palmer is an extraordinary individual that was chosen and given the opportunity to give God glory and to be a witness of His love, favor, grace and enduring mercy. I am glad to be called his friend. I am favored to be a part of his life along with his wife Tracy as they embark in territories that He has ordained for them for this time and season.

Until the next time, my friend always and forever.

Kimberly Johnson

A Tough Pill to Swallow

It was a cold and dreary night…well that's how I felt when I heard that my friend of over 20 years was laying in the hospital bed fighting for his life. When I saw him lying there with tubes coming out of his mouth, I wanted to cry and scream. How could a man that was healthy as a horse, become so ill? I learned quickly that it was not my pill to swallow, but it was my duty to get on my knees and pray until Heaven fell for his healing. The bible says in Psalm 119:71 (NIV), "It was good for me to be afflicted so that I might learn your decrees."

I never understood that bible verse until I saw my dear friend talking and being a witness to how he would go through this again, just to win souls for Christ. I am a strong believer in God and His healing power. I am a confident believer that Pastor Michael Palmer was born to win!

Owunya L. Drake

INTRODUCTION

It Is Good That I Was Afflicted!
"Pain is 'legal tender' that qualifies you for the next destination in your life" (M. Palmer)

Let me first say this: If it had not been for the LORD bringing me out of my affliction (Psalm 34:19), I would not be alive to write about it! To HIM I attribute all the credit and the glory!

You may ask the question, "Have you lost your mind? Why would you call 'affliction' a good thing?" Well, I'm glad you asked these two questions! As to the first question, YES!!! I've completely lost MY mind! My experience, though very traumatic, painful, and something that I wouldn't wish upon my worst enemy, caused me to make a necessary exchange…….a mind (spiritual) exchange as it were! I realized that in order for me to achieve the next level and destination of my life and my family's life, experience things that I've never experienced before, go places that I've never been before, and stand on platforms that I've never graced before, it was going to cost me something! Money couldn't pay for it, charm and wits wouldn't cut it, college degrees and accolades wouldn't satisfy the fee. PAIN/AFFLICTION was the only legal tender that would satisfy payment to be able to advance to the next destination in my life! I know you may not want to hear this solid truth, but the same may hold true for you…that is, if you desire to go to the next place in your life where God has designed for you to be. The purpose of this book is to educate people on the severity of the medical condition that I experienced as well as to encourage someone on how to not "get stuck" on your journey but actually "go through" your experience so that you can reach your destination. I will be chronicling various details of my experiences and doing my best to reconcile the lessons I've learned (naturally and spiritually) with how I was able to allow the process to enable me…….not disable me!

I was thinking of the best way to breakdown various stages of my experiences, so I decided to use something that all of us HAVE TO experience whether we want to or not. As long as we are alive, every last one of us will experience and endure SEASONS! That's right, fall, winter, spring, and summer. Each one has unique attributes and some are embraced more than the other. However, whether it is the falling off of things in the fall, the death of things in the winter, the rebirth of things in the spring, or even the "fun-in-the-sun" of summer, I have found this to be true,..all four seasons are necessary and have purpose on this planet! As you read this book, it is my prayer that you will re-examine your seasons and the conditions they have rendered, and be able to discover the God-given necessity of each season.

FALL
The Beginning of Pain

As I begin to reflect on my road to recovery, especially while having to be inside my home for months during a very dismal polar vortex, I couldn't help but look out my living room window and watch the snowflakes fall endlessly. In Indianapolis, Indiana, the city and state where I live, we were continuously pounded by multiple days of sub-zero temperatures, howling winds, and historic snow falls. It literally shut the city down! This was the winter of 2013/14. While watching the events of winter occur, I remember thinking that, although it seems as if winter was going to last forever, it would have to give way to the NEXT SEASON! This is why placing my experiences within the seasons is very palatable. While continuing to witness the blistery conditions outside, I began to ponder as to why such harsh events had to occur? After all, most vehicular fatalities occur during this season. Many people die from hypothermia. Shelters become overly-capacitated during this time! As I pondered these things and God's purpose for this cold, dead season, it was as if "Winter" replied to my inquiry and said, "before you ponder on me too much, you may want to ponder on the season that arrived before me…..Fall!" That is exactly what I did. I began to look back over the previous years' events that I went through and matched them with the unique attributes of the four seasons, beginning with Fall.

As we already know, Fall (also called Autumn) marks the transition from Summer to Winter. It is often thought of as one of the most colorful and adored seasons by some people. Its bright colors create such beauty, almost as if God Himself took a paint brush and began a beautiful piece of artwork! However, the truth is that, though fall is celebrated largely due to its glaring beauty, especially on the leaves, it only lasts for a short time. You see, in the fall the arrival of night becomes noticeably earlier and the temperature cools considerably, leading to the inevitable……the shedding/the falling off of leaves from deciduous trees (trees designed to lose its leaves). This is due to the change in atmosphere. Some philosophers refer to this change as the "groaning of nature's pain."

The beginning of my experience very much reminded me of this season. I can remember, months before being hospitalized and operated on, just receiving a clean bill of health from the doctor. I was the picture of health! I worked out 3 to 4 times a week. I ate a very sensible diet. I was very active! I remember celebrating my wife's birthday on July 22, 2013 at a local restaurant, having a blast as we normally do when we're together. While at the restaurant, I remember stretching my back out as to loosen it up a bit. I always had a little stiffness in my back. However, I didn't think anything of it at the time, so we went on about our day. A few days before, I played at a concert where I had to carry some musical equipment around. The equipment was rather heavy, but I moved it without any trouble. Shortly after my wife's birthday, I noticed a more-than-usual discomfort in my lower back. Even at that time, I didn't think much about the pain. After all, I recently did some heavy lifting and perhaps my back was a little sore because of it. One day, I remember running an errand and when I returned home, it was a little physically taxing getting out of the car. I went inside and asked my wife to examine my lower back to see if there was anything on the surface of my skin. She didn't feel or see anything. The next day, I had a wedding rehearsal to attend for a good friend of mine. While climbing into my truck, I still felt a little discomfort in my lower back and when I arrived to the rehearsal, exiting my truck proved to be a little more difficult than usual. While sitting on the organ bench during rehearsal, I noticed how uncomfortable it was to sit. So after rehearsal, I braved the entry and exit of my truck, returned home, and asked my wife to re-examine my lower back. Of course, my wife, being the loving woman she is, put me on her "radar" from this point on! I had another rehearsal to attend within a few days....two rehearsals in fact. After my second rehearsal, I remember, during the drive back home, stopping by the store to buy a few things. Suddenly, while in the store, I started to have chills and flu-like tenderness all over my body so I immediately left, braved the entry and exit of my car and returned home. My wife examined me and discovered I had a fever and the area above my tailbone was reddish and inflamed. By this time, it was as if the tenderness I felt all over my body heightened my lower back pain as well as the pain in my buttocks. It was extremely painful! Saturday, July 27th was the day of the wedding I was going to play for. Once I sat on the organ bench, the pain began to return, however, I made it through the wedding. Immediately after the wedding was over, I went home, changed clothes, and my wife and I went to the Emergency Room (ER). If you have ever been to the ER, you ALREADY KNOW that you're going to be there for HOURS before your name is called! Your head could be barely hanging from your neck and your arm could be falling off your shoulder, and YOU'RE STILL GOING TO BE WAITING! Well, I know that all hospitals aren't like that, but on that day, IT WAS LIKE THAT! One hour…2 hours…3 hours went past. All the while, I'm finding a great degree of difficulty in comfortably sitting in those already-hard seats in ER! Once my name was finally called, the medical personnel examined my lower back with her hand, without actually looking at the spot that was inflamed above my tailbone. You see, once she touched my lower back, it was so inflamed that she thought the area she was touching was where my pain originated. We tried to explain that there was an area right above the tailbone that was a bit reddish and inflamed, but she didn't want me to undress so she could see what we were talking about. So, after waiting many hours to be seen and so-called examined, all she did was prescribe muscle relaxers and pain medication and suggested I see a Spine Specialist for follow-up!

The next day we went to church. I was still in pain, but it was a little more manageable. As usual, after church, we ate Sunday dinner, prepared the kids' clothes for the first day of the new school year, and went to bed so we would be ready for the next day. When morning came and it was time for me to get the kids ready for school, I could hardly move! I told my wife that she was going to have to take my daughter to school because I simply didn't have the strength to do it. It was like something had zapped all of my strength overnight! So, Tracy got the kids ready, drove my daughter to school, and then went to the pharmacy to pick up my pain medicine. At this point, all I wanted to do was lay down and rest. Not only was my energy gone, but my appetite was decreasing as well. Now, I'm a Palmer, and Palmers LOVE to eat, so something was definitely wrong! I took the pain medicine, but it didn't really work. The next day, I stayed in bed for most of the day. *My leaves were beginning to change colors.* Wednesday came and I still was unable to leave the apartment, so my parents came over to visit me for a while. That morning, my wife made a doctor's appointment through a different health network to get a second opinion as to what was going on with me. Thankfully, we were able to get an appointment for the very next day, which was Thursday, August 1st. How often does that happen? Due to the excruciating pain I was in, my wife had to drive me to my appointment. It was so painful to exit the car that she had to bring a wheelchair to the car and help me out of the car. It was even more painful to sit in the wheelchair. *My leaves were becoming even more deciduous.* Once the doctor CORRECTLY examined me, she immediately noticed a growth right above my tailbone area which she described as being an abscess. She then gave me the option of getting it lanced in the office or go home and take "sitz" baths which would drain the abscess. The doctor also prescribed a different pain medication and antibiotics to treat any potential infection.

The following morning, I was walking from my bedroom to the living room. As I passed the kitchen where my daughter was sitting and eating breakfast, she looked at me with a very, unusually strange demeanor on her face. She made a comment about my face looking scary. When my wife saw my face, she agreed. Of course, I didn't notice anything different about my face, but according to Tracy, she said that it was sunken in and very dark. She said that it resembled someone who was dying. "You had the look of death on your face," she explained. Later that morning, I went to the bathroom to weigh myself and noticed that I had lost 12 pounds from the time I was just at the doctor's office yesterday! While in the bathroom, I felt the sensation that my bladder was full, however while trying to urinate, nothing would come out! My wife came to the bathroom to check on me. She mentioned that I was complaining of being dehydrated and needing an I.V. She also mentioned that I could not keep my balance while in the bathroom. Obviously, I was unaware of my lack of balance. She had to help me stand so that I would not fall. I was lethargic and it was causing me to think and act below my normal capacity. *My leaves were falling and discoloring…giving way to my next season….winter.*

Shortly thereafter, my wife contacted my parents to notify them that something was not right with me. Of course my mom and dad, being the loving parents they are rushed over to see about me. When my dad saw me, he asked Tracy if I was wearing a heat pack on my right buttock. She answered, "No. His right buttock is swollen!" Of course, as you can imagine, my dad was pretty shocked to see this. His baby boy has never been in this condition before. At this point, my coherency began to come and go. My wife had called to see if the doctor could see me immediately or if we should go to the ER. Something was not right with me! Initially, I had no recollection of my parents actually coming back to my apartment, but they were there. In fact, since I could no longer walk on my own, my dad had to help me get into the car. Once again, when we arrived to the doctor's office, my wife had to bring a wheelchair to the car to get me to the waiting area. This time, the same nurse that escorted us to the exam room had noticed something. She said, "Mr. Palmer, I noticed you're not complaining of any pain while sitting in the wheelchair this time!" You see, the reason why I could not feel any pain while sitting in the wheelchair this time was because the flesh around the site of my abscess had already began to die (necrotize). Dead flesh has no sensation. This is the very last comment that I can actually recall. I was slipping into unconsciousness. I was becoming even more unresponsive. *I was dying. All of my leaves were just about on the ground…discolored… brittle...dying.* Tracy told me that, during that same appointment, when the doctor examined me this time, the swelling of my right buttock was very obvious. It was extremely large. In the doctor's words, she said, "This is not the same man I just examined yesterday! You need to rush him to the emergency room immediately!" Due to my lethargy and incoherency experienced at the time, I've asked my wife to give you her accounts from her recollection of these rapidly-occurring events…..

A Day I Will Never Forget….. Tracy's Story

"What happened?" That was the question I found myself answering over and over again ever since Friday, August 2, 2013…

Shortly after my birthday, July 22, 2013, I remember Michael saying he had a pain in his lower back that was making him uncomfortable. As each day went by, that pain became more and more intense, so Michael would have me look at the area to see if there was a growth back there. Since I am "Dr. Tracy," I decided to go online and do some research on pain in that area. Based on my research it seemed that he possibly had some type of cyst growing deep below the skin that hadn't surfaced yet. So I started putting really warm heating packs over the area to help ease the pain and to try and bring it to surface.

If you know Michael Anthony Palmer, Sr., you know that he won't allow any pain or sickness to slow him down from his hustle! But by the evening of Friday, July 26th, he had developed a fever, had flu-like symptoms, and that area right above the tailbone had become a bit red and inflamed. It definitely wasn't a typical lower back pain, something more concerning was going on, but of course we had no clue as to what it could be. At this point, I have to admit, I was a bit worried. I remember crying and praying over him. I hated seeing him in that much pain and discomfort and we couldn't figure out why. Since he had a wedding to play for the next day, he decided to just take some pain medicine and rest that evening and see how he would feel in the morning. When he got up Saturday morning, the fever and flu-like symptoms were gone but the lower back pain was still a bit intense. So after taking the kids to the dentist and then playing for the wedding, we decided to go to the closest hospital's Emergency Room to get checked out. After hours spent in the waiting room and a less than thorough exam from the medical assistant, my husband was sent home with a prescription for pain medication and muscle relaxers! Really??? So that's your diagnosis??? The medical assistant didn't even have him undress to examine the area we said was inflamed and reddish. She just assumed based off the symptoms we described and a little push on the back, that it must be a pulled muscle and recommended he see a

Spine Specialist for follow up! Now looking back at the situation we know God's hand was in that moment because that wasn't the hospital that Michael was supposed to be admitted to.

Monday, July 29th was the first day back to school for our kids and normally Michael would get them up and ready for school, but he was in so much pain when he woke up he could barely move. Over the next couple of days his appetite severely decreased, pain meds weren't really working, he laid around a lot not leaving the apartment, basically he just wasn't himself. At this point we were both a bit emotional about the situation because Michael doesn't stay down like this for days at a time. He wasn't interacting with me or the kids much because the pain and the medication (I had assumed at the time) kept him lying around or sleep. It was hard on all of us, and all I could say was "God, what is going on?" By Wednesday morning, I suggested that we try and get an appointment through the hospital network I was a part of (which is St. Vincent Hospital), and to my surprise they scheduled him an appointment for the very next day as a new patient. I know that was the favor of God because I have never been able to get an appointment that quickly!

On the day of his appointment, after helping Michael in and out of the tub, I noticed that the inflamed area above his tailbone had begun to form what looked like a cyst or abscess. Obviously the moisture and heat from the bath finally drew it to surface. At that moment I felt that maybe the doctor would probably lance or drain it and he would finally have his pain relieved. The doctor did diagnose it as cellulitis and an abscess and gave the option for him to just do some sitz baths to let it drain on its own. She also prescribed a different pain medication and some antibiotics. Once we got back home and he got settled and rested a few hours, he noticed that the pain had moved from above the tailbone area to his right thigh. That seemed a bit weird but we didn't think much more about it.

Friday, August 2, 2013 is a day I will never forget….. It was time to get the kids up and ready for school, so I started my day like I had done all week. Michael had gone to bed extremely early the night before, only waking up to take medicine. He had a full schedule of rehearsals, a wedding, and other services to play for that weekend, but he had been laid up in excruciating pain all week. How was he going to do all that? So I woke him up and told him he needed to get out the bed and move around to show me if he was well enough for the full weekend ahead. I wasn't prepared for what happened next. When he finally got out of the bed and headed towards the living room, the look of death was all over his face. His face was thin and sunken in and eyes looked like they were bulging out. When he walked past my daughter she said, "Whoa, daddy's face looks scary!" And she was right, he really looked bad. Once he sat down on the couch, I fixed him something to eat so that he could take his medicine and then I left to take our daughter to school. When I returned, I noticed that he didn't eat any of his food. When I asked him why he didn't eat, his response was "I didn't?" Then I noticed that he was breathing faster than normal and I asked him why was he breathing so fast and his response was "I am?" Ok, at this point I do not like the way he is looking and responding to me and it's got me worried. While on the couch, he was very drowsy and not able to stay woke. I began to wonder if maybe he was having an allergic reaction to all the pain meds that he had been taking. I kept watching him and thinking, maybe I need to call the doctor and have Michael seen again. When he got off the couch to use the bathroom, I decided to follow him to make sure he was okay. While in the bathroom I noticed he was still breathing fast, not able to keep his balance while standing, and not able to urinate. The back of the shorts he was wearing were also wet in the area where the abscess was. I figured it finally drained but then I noticed that his upper right buttock was extremely swollen which made it look like he was standing crooked or slanted. As he began to talk his speech was more slurred and unclear then he started mumbling about needing an IV because he felt dehydrated. At this point I am going into full panic mode and I heard the spirit of the Lord tell me to call the doctor immediately! It was an urgency like I have never felt before. You may say, "well common sense would tell you to call" (and that is true too) but if you have ever felt the spirit of God urge you to do something, then you know exactly the feeling I am talking about!

I quickly called the doctor's office and began to explain to the receptionist what was going on and that we needed to get him in the office immediately or I need to take him to the ER. She put me on hold to speak to the doctor's nurse and they told me to get him in within the next few hours. As soon as I got off the phone with the receptionist, I called Michael's parents to let them know what was going on, and then I contacted both of the kids' schools to let them know I was on my way to pick them up early. When I went back to the bedroom to check on Michael he was almost hyperventilating, still not responding well, and drifting in and out of consciousness. I began to pray over him and calm him down so that I could leave to go pick up the kids. Once he started to calm down and focus more, I told him I needed to leave to pick up the kids from school because I was taking him back to the doctor and he needed to get ready and put his shoes on while I was gone. Since his parents were only minutes away, I knew he wouldn't be at the apartment alone for long. When I got back home from picking up the kids, his parents were already there and Michael was sitting in the living room. His father had to help him walk up the steps and get into the car because he could barely keep his balance or walk straight. While driving to the doctor's office, I just kept talking to him and trying to keep him alert and responsive. Once we got him into the doctor's office, she looked at him and recognized that his condition had severely changed in 24 hours. He was not the same person she saw just yesterday and she instructed us to immediately take him to the hospital ER and she was going to call them to let them know we were heading over there. When we arrived there was a security guard that brought a wheelchair out to the car and helped put Michael in it and took him in the waiting room for us. Since Michael was still going in and out of consciousness, I had to answer all the intake questions the nurse was asking. It wasn't long before he was taken into an exam room and the doctor examined him, had his blood drawn, and ran tests. The results showed that his blood glucose level was 787, he was in diabetic ketoacidosis, had acute kidney injury (failure), and was going into septic shock due to a severe infection. This means that my husband's immune system began to overwhelmingly respond to the infection in his body which began to cause his organs to fail and if not treated immediately, would lead to a coma and possibly death. Medically speaking, my husband was dying… but God!

Immediately the medical staff began to make arrangements to move him to the Intensive Care Unit (ICU). While waiting for them to get him a room, I was busy filling out insurance & medical paperwork, went to the waiting room to let his parents & siblings know what was going on, sent out a few text messages and made a few phone calls to family, friends, pastors, etc.. letting them know what was going on with Michael. Even though I heard what the doctor said and I knew Michael was going to be admitted into ICU, for some reason it didn't really sink in at the time that my husband was really sick and could die! In my mind I was thinking that we may be here for a few days while they get the blood sugar down and treat the infection and then everything will go back to normal and be just fine. But what happened next changed our lives forever….

Once they got him settled in his room, the nurses were working around the clock to get his blood sugar down as quickly as possible. The doctor's felt at the time it was important to get the blood sugar more stable before they could take him to surgery to remove the abscess. So all we could do was patiently wait. Meanwhile several friends, family members, ministers/pastors came out to visit and pray with him that evening. It was a little sad seeing him not that responsive and not his talkative self as people were visiting him. As the evening grew later, people started to leave and the only ones still at the hospital with me were my cousin and a friend from church. Michael's parents took the kids home with them so they didn't have to stay and wait all night at the hospital.

It had to be 10:00 or 10:30 pm when the surgeon wanted to speak with me. He began to explain that he felt Michael needed to go to surgery immediately because he believed the infected area was making it difficult for his blood sugar to stabilize more quickly. He said that the procedure should only take about 45 minutes and they were going to begin prepping him for surgery. Once I gave my consent for them to begin surgery, we headed downstairs to the operating room waiting area. While down there I sent out a few text messages letting people know he was headed to emergency surgery and to be in prayer. When the message got to Michael's mom she headed right back out to the hospital.

So there we were, all four of us, patiently waiting for the surgery to begin and end. There was a monitor in the waiting room area to let you know when the surgery procedure began, when the procedure was almost finished, and when the patient was in recovery. So of course I am watching this screen every few minutes to see what was going on. It may have been about 12:00 a.m. Saturday morning, and every time I looked at the screen it showed his name, but it didn't indicate that the surgery procedure had begun. I figured that either they got a late start or the screen wasn't updated yet. Time just seemed to go by so slow but I kept checking the screen until finally it showed that the procedure had started. It may have been after 12:30 a.m. or so by this time. Since the doctor said that the surgery should only take about 45 minutes, I tried to wait at least an hour before checking the screen again. When I did look at the screen again, it said that the surgery was still in progress. Ok, I am a little nervous but I know how surgeries can sometimes take longer than expected. So I waited another 30 minutes. Still in progress. More time passed. STILL in progress. More time passed. STILL IN PROGRESS. By now it's about 3:30 am and the surgery is still in progress and no one has come out to say anything! I am a complete nervous wreck by now! I can't stop pacing the floor, stomach is in knots, feeling shaky, wondering what in the world is going on! Somebody please tell me something! Finally, out comes the operating room nurse to let us know that Michael was still in surgery but he was stable and the surgeons should be finishing up soon. At that moment I felt a bit of relief but I was told that this surgery should only take 45 minutes and it's been well over 3 hours!

By now I have calmed down enough to sit still and to my surprise I actually dosed off. I am not sure how long I slept but I was awaken abruptly by my friend from church when she saw three doctors in white coats coming towards us. As the two gentlemen and one lady approached us I started to feel those butterflies in my stomach. "Ok Tracy, prepare yourself for whatever they have to say," I whispered to myself. As they sat down in front of us, the surgeon I met with in the ICU began to speak first. He let me know that Michael was still stable and the other operating room staff was finishing up the procedure. He then began to explain why the procedure had taken so long; Michael had a flesh-eating bacteria caused by an infection called Necrotizing Fasciitis. This infection was so aggressive that when they would remove one area of dead tissue, more would die, then as they removed another area, even more would die, to the point the infection ate all the way down to the muscle and exposed his hip bone. As you can imagine I am in complete shock at that moment. I believe my mind went blank for a moment and all I could do was just stare and nod and say okay. Then he continued explaining that it was so aggressive that it began to eat away down to the muscle, so he had to immediately call in the orthopedic surgeon (which was the male surgeon that was sitting next to him). The orthopedic surgeon explained that when he entered the operating room he had to remove quite a bit of the muscle tissue in the right buttock and thigh area.

(Let me pause right here because I want to give you a more accurate "medical" understanding of what went on in the operating room according to the doctor's written report…. According the report, when the first surgeon (Dr. Jacobson) began to cut into Michael's right buttock to remove the infected abscess, it began to liquefy and released an exceptionally foul smelling odor. The more they removed the outer layer of skin and fat tissue that was necrotic, the surgeon noticed it had begun to eat away at the entire gluteus maximus muscle of the right buttock. When this happens it's called myonecrosis which means "muscle tissue death." This usually results in the loss of movement and amputation or fatality is fairly common. Since the muscle tissue was affected, Dr. Jacobson had to call in the orthopedic surgeon and he used special equipment to remove the muscle tissue that was necrotic. He had to completely or partially remove the thigh muscles that are important for walking, controlling balance, leg extension, movement of muscle, and rotating the hip because they were all necrotic. So now I hope you have a better idea of how serious this was.)

Ok back to my story…. As they continued to talk they said they believed that they got most of it but since it was so aggressive it could continue to eat away at the flesh and that Michael would probably need several more surgeries. They also mentioned that since such a large amount of flesh and tissue was removed he would need lots of reconstructive surgery done, which would include adding artificial flesh. (According to the doctor's written report, the wound size was about 25cm x 18 cm in width or 450cm2.) After they finished explaining everything to us, I managed to ask the question "Will he be able to walk again?" They said "if" he is able to walk again, he will have a permanent limp. All I could whisper was "ok." By this time I must have been in so much shock that they had to ask me if I understood everything they were telling me and if I would be okay. I just nodded and then they threw the final blow. They said when you see your husband he will be in an induced coma and on a ventilator. (During the surgery his blood pressure dropped, his heart rate increased and he developed acute respiratory failure-according to the doctor's written report) He was also on a Wound V.A.C. (Vacuum Assisted Closure) which is a machine that would help tremendously with the healing process of the large wound. After they said how sorry they were and told us we could go back upstairs to the ICU waiting area, they finally left. I heard voices around me saying "let's go back upstairs," but when I stood up I just froze, put my hands over my face, and whispered "Jesus." Immediately my friend put her arms around me and began to speak encouraging words and prayed for me. When I could finally get my legs to move, we all headed back upstairs.

It had to be after 5:00 a.m. and all I could do was pace the hallways back and forth since I was too jittery to sit still. "God, this is a bit much to handle right now. It wasn't supposed to be like this. Why didn't I know he was this sick? What is really happening right now!" I was feeling extremely sick to my stomach, dizzy, confused, exhausted…just a mess! Michael's mom put her arms around me and said everything would be just fine, even though she was trying to deal with this shocking news as well. The more we waited for them to take Michael back to his room, the more I realized I wasn't ready to see him on a ventilator. I decided I needed to go home and get some rest so I could wrap my mind around all this. Michael's mom, my cousin, and friend from church decided to stay because they wanted to see him, but I just wasn't ready.

I promise that was the longest and most exhausting drive I have ever made in my life! It seemed like it took me hours to make a 40 minute drive. It was raining, I was unfocused, and very exhausted since I had been up for over 24 hours. I was even confused at how to get home! Lord Help Me! When I finally got home all I could do was say in a very loud voice, "God you need to tell me what's going on! I need to know if my husband is going to die or what because this one has caught me off guard!" I continued to cry out to God for answers until I finally fell asleep. A couple of hours passed and I believe the spirit of the Lord woke me up and I was speaking in tongues, then a peace came over me like never before. God began to reveal to me that Michael wasn't going to die and I would see the glory of God through this situation. God also showed me a vision of people praying and the Lord said to me that never had so many people come together on one accord at one time to pray for one person and I am releasing my healing power on Michael. (Later, I discovered that Michael received a similar vision from God while he was in ICU.) After this encounter with God, I was more than ready to go back to the hospital to see my husband. I also put a message on Facebook and sent a text to family and friends updating them on his condition. On my way back to the hospital, I stopped over Michael's parent's house to drop off a change of clothes for the kids and to take Michael's dad and the kids back out to the hospital with me.

When I walked in Michael's room, it was such a peace and a calm presence in there. I began to feel a strength that only God could give. I was determined that as long as I was there, no one was going to come in that room doubtful or fearing, but have a positive attitude and faith! I knew that God was about to perform a miracle right before our very eyes! From the time Michael was admitted into ICU on Friday, August 2nd, he became known as the most popular patient at the hospital. I believe he had hundreds of visitors that came and showed their love and support during that very challenging time. Even the nurses and doctors were amazed at all the love, support and faith that was shown towards him. They kept saying, "He must be a very special guy!" Yes he is!

From Friday, August 2nd to Sunday, August 4th, I was at the hospital day and night except when I left for several hours early Saturday morning. That weekend was challenging because even though he was stable, he was still very sick and the doctor's weren't sure if he would survive. His blood sugar was coming down slowly but still high, heart rate was still high, needed quite a few blood transfusions, was on medication to keep his blood pressure up, had a fever, on a ventilator, in a coma, etc… But I had a word from the Lord that "he shall live and not die!" By Sunday evening I knew I had to finally leave the hospital and take my kids home since they had to go back to school on Monday. As much as I didn't want to leave my husband's side, I had children to raise and a household to run until my "king" came back home. As the kids and I were getting in the car preparing to leave, my daughter said, "Wait mommy we can't leave, daddy isn't with us." Oh my goodness, when she said that it hurt me to the core. At that moment reality set in, my husband isn't coming home anytime soon. Michael always comes home…. The drive home was very silent except for the music playing in the background. When I finally got home, got out the car, and walked through the doors, the first thing I saw was a family photo on the wall and at that moment I broke down crying. My daughter ran to her room and fell on her bed and began to cry uncontrollably. When I finally made it from the living room to my bedroom I just sat on the bed and wept. Then the most amazing thing happened, my son, who was 12 years old at the time, put his arms around me and began to pray. When I say that my son prayed, I mean he prayed! As he was praying, my 7 year old daughter came in the room and he put his arm around her and continued to comfort us both. He became the spiritual leader of the household at that very moment. Only God could have done that!

From the time Michael was hospitalized until he was discharged from rehabilitation on October 24th, 2013, we witnessed the miraculous healing power of God in Michael's life. I watched this life-threatening infection not only take a large amount of flesh from his body, but it stripped him of all his physical strength and his ability to walk, but I serve a God that specializes in the area of restoration! My husband was moved from Intensive Care Unit to a regular room after only being there for a week. This was weeks earlier than what the doctors had expected. His flesh began to grow back faster than they had ever seen before. He began to regain his strength and ability to walk much sooner than expected. (I remember when Michael had his final surgery to remove any remaining necrotizing flesh, I asked the surgeon how long would it be before Michael would possibly get back to his normal routine and get off the wound V.A.C. machine. The surgeon said in order for Michael to even do half of what he used to do, it would take at least 6 months to

1 year!) Well, 4 months later, that same doctor was removing the wound V.A.C. permanently and doing my husband's final skin graft surgery! A few months after that my husband was walking on a cane, driving, and returning to most of his normal activities! To God be the glory!

Those 12 weeks of him being in the hospital and rehab were extremely tough at times, but God truly kept his loving arms around us. There were times I blamed myself for not insisting that he went to a doctor or the hospital sooner and maybe we could have caught it before it got so bad, but then I realized that God's hand was in the entire situation and He orchestrated it from the beginning to end. If things didn't happen exactly the way they did, you wouldn't be reading this book right now and we wouldn't have the opportunity to minister to other families who are currently going through difficult and life changing situations. "And we know that all things work together for the good of those who love God, and are called according to His purpose." (Romans 8:28) It was all so that the power of God might be made manifested in him and for that we are forever grateful!

WINTER
A Time of Loss

We who live in places that lie between the tropics and the polar region have become very acquainted with this season called winter. It is the season where the weather becomes cold and blustery. The icy conditions make it difficult to navigate through traffic. Vehicles get stuck and people get stranded in places that, in other seasons, they would normally flow smoothly. Oftentimes, schools, churches, and businesses are forced to delay or even close. Popular holidays such as Christmas and New Years Day are celebrated during this season. The equity shared between day and night becomes unevenly divided during this season, yielding the majority of time to the night. This season is where all the leaves that have fallen off of the trees began to crumble and become buried in the ground, seemingly lost for good. However, as previously mentioned, though this season seems to linger, EVENTUALLY even "old man winter" has to give way to the next season! But before the spring can truly emerge with its elegance and colorful beauty, there IS a purpose for winter's howling existence! In fact, the beauty of the spring could not exist without the natural preparations made during the winter! In other words the rebirth experienced, enjoyed, and celebrated in the spring would not exist if not for the death that is necessary during the winter. Winter's blustery conditions oftentimes put you in a position where all you can do is be remote and watch from your window. It will cause you to be put in a place to where you can't go anywhere or do anything. This season certainly reminds me of my experience shortly after being admitted to the hospital. My winter season lasted from August 2, 2013 to August 9, 2013.

During this period of time I was admitted into the Intensive Care Unit. This was a time where I had to undergo a series of emergency surgeries to aggressively attack the flesh-eating bacteria medically known as Necrotizing Fasciitis. This is a rare but very serious disease and usually 1 in 4 people who get this infection dies. I was told that, if I was woke to experience the pain from the type of surgeries that I had undergone, I would have gone into cardiac arrest. You see, the infection caused my body to go into septic shock and my vital organs began to fail. This is one of the main reasons I had to be put in an induced coma, on a ventilator, a heart monitor, etc... My surgeries, as all surgeries, were very serious. In an aggressive effort to debride all of the rapidly progressive flesh-eating bacteria, I lost my entire right buttock along with muscle tissue and flesh, exposing my hip bone (just as my wife explained previously). According to the surgeons and specialists, amputation was not out of the realm of discussion. Because of being on a ventilator so long, the oxygen in my muscles were zapped, causing muscle atrophy. Muscle atrophy is a condition where muscle mass decreases due to the inability to engage in normal physical activity, thus causing extreme weakness, fatigue, and muscle shrinkage. I was so weak that my cell phone was as heavy as a laptop! Due to my acute kidney failure I had to wear a catheter, and I also had to temporarily wear a rectal balloon catheter in order to have bowel movements. They had to feed me through a tube so that I would not aspirate. Since I had to wear a catheter for such an extended amount of time, I developed a urinary tract infection. Also the rectal balloon catheter had been hooked to me for so long that it irritated the rectal walls which caused me to need a colonoscopy…..something that I thought I would not have to deal with until I was at least 45 years of age! The results from the colonoscopy determined that I had developed hemorrhoids. Even though I had a massive amount of waste sitting in my system, which could have caused deadly bacteria to began to form inside of my body, it was a relief to know that hemorrhoids was a minor ailment compared to what it could've been! I lost extreme amounts of blood, coupled with having to wear a wound V.A.C. for my large surgical wound; I also became anemic and required several blood transfusions. This was a very painful time. When a patient has to wear a wound V.A.C., it is because the wound is so large that it cannot be merely sutured like a small surgical wound. The wound V.A.C. is programmed to a specified suction level designed to suction out blood from the wound site as well as promote faster closure of the wound itself. It was even painful to be bathed and painful to move around for bed changes. As if the bed linen changes weren't painful enough, the wound changes proved to be even more brutal. Because I could not just hop out of the bed, the nurses and technicians would have to turn me all the way to one side of the bed to pull the bed sheets from under me. The friction and abrasion caused by the pulling sheets rubbing against my bed-ridden skin pushed my pain level to 10! Then they would have to turn me onto my right side to finish the linen change; the side in which my large surgical wound was. The pain was numbing. Can you imagine someone cutting into your buttocks with a lumberjack's saw and then throwing salt directly into the wound while poking and scraping at the open wound with a large wire brush? The throbbing pain was agonizing and very excruciating. That was an experience I had to endure every day, and that was only the linen changes! The wound changes were another ordeal by itself! As mentioned earlier in this book, my entire right buttocks had to be removed along with a portion of the flesh from my hip and thigh. When you see some of the post-surgical images (shown later in this book), you'll see why my affected area is often described as a shark bite. I remember every other day my surgical wound dressings needing to be changed. You see, after the first surgery, my wound was very large and very deep, and if you were to look at the place where my right buttocks and part of my hip and thigh used to be, you would only see a black hole with my hip bone exposed. So in order for them to properly dress my wound, the wound specialists would have to pack the deep opening of my wound with 7 extra-large thick layers of foam. The pain from these multiple wound changes was TEN TIMES worse than the bed linen changes! It wasn't the application of the new wound dressings that was so excruciating. It was the removal of the old wound dressings that would make any grown man cry like a baby. First, they would have to remove the wound tape that was adhesed to my skin. Then they would have to remove *(more like ripping it off)* all of those pieces of foam that were packed in the large hole of my wound. The first few layers were very painful, but the last layer was a BEAR! This was the layer that had to be pulled directly off of the fresh wound itself! OUCH! I was calling on Jesus, Mama, and anyone else who came to mind! Mildly put, this experience felt like a wax job with gorilla glue and duct tape! After changing my wound with fresh dressings, the last part would involve restarting the wound V.A.C. machine. As if the throbbing from the "wax job" wasn't painful enough, when they restarted the V.A.C., the suction power felt like someone was pinching my entire wound with vice grips! I tell you, I was going through it!

The post-surgical pain from the surgeries was so great that the doctors put me on a medication called *Dilaudid*. It was administered to me through the injection of a PICC line (peripherally inserted central catheter). It has been reported that this drug has up to ten times the potency of another opioid called *heroin.* Never in my life have I taken any kind of narcotic, but while hospitalized this was a remedy to at least control my pain. In addition to other medication that I was on to help control my pain while in ICU, *dilaudid* was the one that I was given almost daily until my discharge. I can recall many hallucinations while on this medication. I remember fighting with bouts of anxiety, feelings of ice-cold loneliness, and being frightened by sights and sounds. I remember feeling as if I would be calling for help, but no one was there to answer me. You know how a fish in an aquarium moves its mouth as if it's saying, "HELP, HELP" but no one ever helps the fish? That's how the drugs made me feel; like I was inside an aquarium on display for people to see me but they couldn't hear me nor help me. My friends, I learned something about that drug. You see, the way *dilaudid* works is it merely changes the way the brain and central nervous system perceive pain and discomfort. Even in the midst of all of my pain and agony, I was able to receive a very simple but profound revelation. Although this drug did what it was designed to do (change my brain's perception of my pain), it taught me that if a synthetic (man-made) remedy could cause me to change the way I perceive my pain, I already had that same ability inside of me to change my perception of pain WITHOUT the narcotic! You see, there was one fact that I would have to face. That was the reality that when I was discharged and went home, this drug wasn't coming home with me. If you can imagine, being weaned off of such a strong drug and being switched to Oxycodone, it was like popping bags of Skittles! It wasn't going to do anything to change any perception of any pain that I would endure once I went home. So I had to find a way to process the pain without the drug. I had to develop the mindset of a Navy SEAL. You see, Navy SEALS get trained on how to endure pain and anguish while maintaining their duties. On September 13, 2011 the *Daily Garriga,* an internet blog, did an article from <u>Men's Health Magazine</u> on "Becoming Mentally Strong :How to Think Like a Navy SEAL." In this article, a Navy SEAL Master Chief was asked how Navy SEALS maintain a high level of productivity while undergoing extreme pain and discomfort. One of the requirements was for a SEAL to develop mental strength. This master chief stated, "The mentally strong individual is one who is not satisfied with just enduring hardship. The mentally strong individual is one who has developed the ability to confront hardship and manifest positive outcomes by exerting POWER OVER CIRCUMSTANCE." This is not a new concept. You can find this verbiage in God's Word in 2 Timothy 2:3 where Paul encourages his understudy Timothy to "Endure hardness (pain, agony, discomfort) as a GOOD SOLDIER of Jesus Christ." My friends let me ask you; what have you been medicating yourself with? What is that vice that you're using as a synthetic substitute to deaden your perception to the reality of your pain and agony? You've been trying different remedies that only work for so long and then you have to "medicate" all over again. Could it be that you've been medicating so long that you've developed a dependency on that synthetic remedy? I have a fact for you, my friends. THE PAIN IS STILL THERE AFTER THE HIGH IS LONG GONE! I would suggest developing your mental strength, and there is one place where I know that you can get the remedies you need in order to go through your affliction with a renewed mindset and clear focus; God's Word! I still have various pains and discomfort from my surgeries, but God's Word has given me the power to renew my mindset and my perception of pain. I've realized that His sufficient grace empowers me with ample capacity to live through the pain. This winter season was in full effect! One thing is for sure, as much as I did not want to encounter ANY of the events of this winter season, if I was going to experience progress, I would have to ENDURE THIS SEASON!

Because of being in ICU for such a long time, I began to experience something call "ICU delirium." This is a condition by which long-term ICU patients begin to hallucinate and act out of character. Yes, I had my episodes of rambunctiousness! ICU delirium also carries a high mortality rate. Oftentimes, brain function begins to rapidly decline and ultimately fail. During this week of being in ICU (of course, not knowing at the time where I was or anything in real time), I experienced very dark, cold, and confusing times. The hallucinations had my mind seemingly all over the place! I remember feeling and thinking that my hospital bed was being transported to a dungeon well below the ground perhaps in or even under a dark basement. Strangely enough, I could hear the beeps and clicks obviously coming from the many machines I was hooked to. It seemed as if I was locked away and could not call for help because I didn't think no one would hear me! I felt isolated from the outside world. In real time, my wife told me that I had many visitors, but of course, I have no recollection of anyone around this time. Although I was in a coma, every-so-often my ears would hasten to the voices of the medical staff while they were working on me and treating me. I recall a nurse asking me to respond to see if I knew where I was. She said, "Mr. Palmer, you are in ICU!" Of course, going through ICU delirium and hallucinations, my mind had produced a scenario of something slightly different than what the nurse uttered in real-time. When she told me that I was in "ICU," my mind produced an image of a chalkboard that spelled out the words "I SEE YOU." Shortly thereafter (in my unconscious mind still), a very nice man came down to the "dungeon" that I thought I was in. He approached the chalkboard and he was dressed in all-white attire. Now, I was in the "dungeon" of a basement by myself. While this man was nearing the chalkboard he kept his eyes locked on mine. The dark basement suddenly looked like a big empty classroom with empty desks surrounding my hospital bed. With his eyes still focused on my eyes and with a big warm and inviting smile on his face, he began to write on the chalkboard. After writing on the chalkboard, he picked up a teacher's pointer and began to point at the board on which he wrote, never once taking his eyes off of me. It was as if he was instructing me on a subject of some sort, but the only thing written on the chalkboard were 3 words which seem to give him the greatest thrill to recite. He read what he had written on the board, "I SEE YOU! I SEE YOU! I SEE YOU!" While feeling kind of anxious and uncertain of any hope of escape from that "dungeon," the joy on this man's face gave me a peace that I cannot recall EVER possessing before in my entire life! I am now convinced that this man was God! I mean, who else has the ability to not only visit you at the hospital, but visit you in your unconscious, delirious, comatose state? None other than the one who laid me in that state for a reason.......so that I could come and visit you who read this book and perhaps are in a state of confusion, feeling cold, alone, and seemingly forgotten. Dear reader, IT IS NOT JUST AN ILLUSION. YOU ARE NOT ALONE!

GOD SAYS, "I SEE YOU! I SEE YOU! I SEE YOU!" He wants me to remind you that your fallen leaves may seem to have no further purpose except to be crumbled and buried, but they do indeed have purpose! You see, those same fallen, crumbled leaves that get covered by the snow becomes fertilizer for the beauty and restoration experienced and enjoyed in your next season......SPRING! You see, your pain is a resource from God, given to you for your enrichment! HE HAS NO WASTED PAIN! Isaiah 55:10-11 confirms my point (NIV): *"As the rain and snow come down from heaven, and do not return to it without watering the earth and making it bud and flourish (the spring), so that it yields seed for the sower and bread for the eater, so is my word that goes out from my mouth: IT WILL NOT RETURN TO ME EMPTY, but it (His Word) WILL ACCOMPLISH what I DESIRE and it (His Word....His will) will achieve the PURPOSE for which I sent it!"* My friends, God NEVER allows loss without gain being on His mind concerning you! As the previous scripture mentioned, God has a plan and a very detailed purpose for your situation. You are not experiencing your issue(s) due to God being caught off guard. He is NEVER in a crisis, and although winter doesn't last forever and definitely will give way to the beauty and restoration of spring, do not become intimidated during the winter!

I'd like to share another vision with you that I had while hospitalized. There was a church located in the middle of a country field. From the outside, the church was nice and quaint. The inside of the sanctuary was designed in a circle. It didn't have a stage or platform. That's where I was. I was the only one in the sanctuary of which seemed to seat about 300 people. However, I was still in my hospital bed surrounded by the sanctuary seats. There were windows that lined the entire sanctuary. They were clear, see-through glass. It was very sunny outside. While looking around the empty sanctuary, people began to file into the sanctuary, filling up all the rows. There were two things I immediately noticed. One thing was that everyone who came in looked at me and greeted me with a very friendly smile. They never said anything; just smiled. The second thing I noticed is that everyone was dressed in the same dark bottoms and the same bright short-sleeved tops. They also greeted one another but still hadn't said a word; just smiled. Then there was a man who entered the sanctuary. I assumed he was the leader of this group of people whom I've never seen before. The next series of events blew my mind. While I was looking to my left and my right I noticed that the people stopped greeting one another. Once this man entered the room, everyone's eyes were fixed on him seemingly awaiting instructions. This man stepped in the middle of the circular sanctuary then lifted his hands and looked up towards the sky, the same way that a baby lifts their hands in desperation when they want mommy or daddy to pick them up. As soon as he lifted his hands, everyone in that sanctuary lifted their hands and looked towards the sky too. No one ever said a word! However, it was as if I could see their prayers of intercession going up to heaven on my behalf. I KNEW they were praying for me! The sanctuary became so bright that I closed my eyes and went to sleep. As I said before, HE SEES YOU, and just like me in that dark, dungeon-like place in my mind during ICU and then in that church sanctuary, He will never take His eyes off of you! He is locked in on you! Spring will come soon enough!

SPRING
Regrowth and Restoration

As we can all attest, the season of spring oftentimes displays a two-part transformation. The first transformation that we witness is the lingering affect and presence of a cold winter. Trees are still void of leaves. We may even still see spots of snow on the ground or even hills of snow that have been piled up by snow plows. The temperature may even be JUST cold enough to still require a coat or heavy jacket. Have you ever been in a winter season so long that even when time and date suggest that seasons have changed and spring has arrived, you still question the existence of a shift in seasons? After all, spring is supposed to display budding branches, colorful flowers, sunshine, fair-tempered weather, and green grass! Spring is supposed to represent and manifest re-growth and restoration! My friends, allow me to encourage those of you who have frequently found or even find yourselves in a mode of questioning if your season of winter has shifted yet. I know it seems to be no budding, no warmth, no re-growth, no restoration or beauty in the thing in which you're going through. You've asked the question, "If spring is here, why do I still feel so cold and abandoned during a time when I should be warm? My sky is still as grey as it was during winter! If this is springtime, where is the proof?" I'm so glad you've asked those questions! In fact, I have some great news! You have only viewed the FIRST transformation of spring! There is still a SECOND PART! My friends, please be reminded of what I told you earlier in this book that God, the creator and expert of ALL seasons, NEVER allows loss (fall and winter) in your life without increase (spring) already being on His mind concerning you! You see, before you can physically witness the manifestation of the re-growth, the beauty and restoration that comes along with the SECOND part of spring, there is one universal, scientific event that has to occur…THAWING! Thawing is a process of something changing or passing from a frozen to a liquid or semi-liquid state. More applicable, it means to be FREED from the effect of frost or extreme cold. In other words, as it pertains to the seasonal shift from winter to spring, and before the ambiance of the SECOND part of spring can be witnessed, the ground MUST go through two things in order for thawing begin……HEAT and TIME! You see, the closer we move towards April and May, the warmer spring becomes. Something begins to occur during this time that has encouraged me during my seasonal shift from winter to spring…..APRIL SHOWERS BRING MAY FLOWERS! However, I'd like to submit that it is not the showers of April that produce the flowers of May. Actually, the rain from "April's showers" play more of an important role in transporting heat from heaven's atmosphere in order to assist in the thawing of the grounds and trees! Well, Mike, what is it then that produces May's flowers and the beauty of the SECOND part of spring? You're not going to believe this, but it is actually the ice, the snow, and the blustery atmosphere of cold air that collides with heaven's rain! And after the ground (you) have "suffered a while," now you are ready to be" made complete, strengthened, and established!" Did you know that when the bible speaks of "earth," it was referring to you? God had you in His mind when he stated in Genesis 8:22, "As long as the earth (you) remains, there will be seed time and harvest, cold and heat, summer and winter…" Dear reader, please understand that both the freezing of the winter and spring's beginning were both in the plan of your Creator. His blueprint for your life is flawless! It's only when we, who being full of flaws, totally yield to His drawn plans, will then completely understand and embrace the affliction while under construction. Just know that the finished work will be something to behold and it will bring glory to His name! One thing that I'd like to put on your mind is, regardless if you like winter or not, with or without your participation or perspective, it is going to snow, it will get icy, and yes, winter may even disable you and shut you down. I'm not a meteorologist, nor do I play one on television, but I CAN give you this immutable prediction…WINTER WON'T LAST FOREVER! THE BEAUTY OF SPRING IS INEVITABLE! Favorable conditions are within the forecast!

I've talked a lot about the beauty and restoration of spring. And although much of spring's beauty is naturally witnessed simply because of natural occurrence, much of its true beauty and appreciation come with a bit of work on our part. After I began to recover and progress from multiple surgeries, I was now healthy and strong enough to be upgraded and moved to the rehabilitation floor of the hospital. The type of physical therapy that I was about to undergo was somewhat of an advanced rehabilitation program from what I was used to. I would be challenged to endure 3 hours a day of physical therapy as well as occupational therapy. This is where I truly experienced part 1 and part 2 of my springtime shift. This is where my true post-operative physical limitations would be exposed. Up until this time of hospitalization, I was restricted to only doing most of my physical therapy while in my hospital bed. The small amount of therapy I did outside of my hospital bed required the staff to connect me to a special lifting device called a "sabina" that hoisted me out of the bed like a crane at a construction site.

On the rehabilitation floor, Monday-Friday, starting at 6am, it was all about strengthening and endurance training. My physical therapy consisted of gruesome wheelchair-to-walker gait workouts, standing exercises, parallel bars, distance walking with a walker,etc...Well, at the beginning I would scoot more than walk! What was even more difficult was to learn how to walk while suffering from "drop foot." With drop foot, you don't have the ability to flex your foot back and forth. To paint a clearer picture, the function between your foot and ankle that allows one to press down on the gas pedal while driving, or the function which allows one to push off while walking or jumping is lost. So when I began learning how to properly use a walker, the physical therapist would have to attach a gait belt around my foot to manually lift my foot while I walked to prevent me from tripping over myself, causing further damage. It was very difficult learning how to walk all over again especially with outside devices, but I was determined to walk again. You see, had I given into the notion of being tired, fatigued, in pain, and just refused to press forward, I would've continued to suffer muscle atrophy and my muscles would've rendered me wheelchair bound. Not a chance! I've already been through winter! It's spring season! It was time for me to re-grow and rebuild strength! My friends, Let me ask….. Do you want to walk again? How bad do you want it? Are you willing to make "fatigue" your friend and "pain" your partner? If so, step 1 is to GET UP! STRETCH YOUR FAITH! Step 2: REPEAT STEP 1!

The other part of my rehabilitation was occupational therapy. This is where I used weightlifting to gain strength and to recover lost muscle mass. This is also where I began learning how to regain balance, coordination, and re-sharpen motor skills. I began to get stronger and delayed motor skills began to return to me over time, but there were two tests that were required of me to pass before I could graduate and be discharged from my 3 month stay at the hospital. First, I had to demonstrate the physical ability to lift myself from a sitting position on the floor onto the training table without the assistance of any device or person. I thought to myself, "this is something I've done all of my life!" However, when you have been disengaged from any normal physical activity for the period of time that I had been, the simple becomes very difficult and extremely complicated! It took me a while to get my mind wrapped around how I was going to lift myself from this floor to another level and accomplish this milestone ahead of me. After numerous failed attempts, I stopped to gather myself and regroup. You see, there were other patients in rehabilitation who were watching me, ones who witnessed me progress through challenge after challenge and my victories helped them overcome some of their own physical challenges. I didn't mind them watching me fail, but I sure was not about to let them see me give up! So, true to my conviction and determination, I gathered the strength to accomplish the task! Does this sound like you? Have you ever been in a challenging situation in your life that has seemingly "floored" you? There was no device or assistance around that you could depend on to help you move from one level to the next? Perhaps you're a single mom who's been laid off or demoted. You were already struggling financially and now your month is even longer than your money. Regardless, your children still expect you to provide for them. Maybe you're a business owner, and due to the economy and slowing demand for your product, business is down. You can barely make payroll, and lay-offs are seemingly inevitable. Whatever situation that has "floored" you, I want you to know that LIFE HAPPENS! Just know that, due to integrity, work ethic, and character you have displayed in front of others in the past, you have been called from the sidelines by the coach (GOD) because He knew that, in order for others around you to accomplish and achieve things in their lives, they're going to have to see victory come from you! It's ok to let them see you fail, but never let it be said that YOU GAVE UP!

The second requirement for graduation and discharge was the challenge of stair climbing! I could barely walk with a walker, and now y'all want me to climb stairs? Here we go again! I knew that if I was going to go home, I would have to prove my ability to climb multiple levels of stairs! As big of a challenge as this seemed to me, it made perfect sense! You see, before I could even get to the front door of my apartment, it required me to first take the stairs! After all, an elevator in the hospital would serve no purpose once I got home! I don't have an elevator in my home. Is there another life application coming? I'm glad you asked! In life, you'll find that, though it requires more effort to reach your destination, IT IS OFTENTIMES BETTER TO TAKE THE STAIRS THAN THE ELEVATOR TO GET THERE! An elevator may get you there faster, but you'll gain so much more strength and endurance from the "steps" in life that will move you from one level to the next! Well, after nervously gathering the courage to attempt the challenge, I DID IT! I had accomplished it! In fact, after accomplishing the challenge, I requested to do it again, and again, and again! I want to encourage you that, whatever the challenge set before you, it can be accomplished! Once you achieve it, go and achieve it again, and again, and again! I had to show other patients and perhaps even you that the expert (God) would NEVER test you without already knowing that you could pass the test! You see, FAITH THAT CAN'T BE TESTED, IS FAITH THAT CAN'T BE TRUSTED!

Well, I made it back home to my beautiful wife and children, and though I have re-gained quite a bit of strength and muscle tone, I still had a ways to go. I still had to go through wound changes, physical & occupational therapy, and home healthcare. However, I was too far into the trip to turn around and give up now! I continued getting stronger by continuing to lift weights, stretch, eat healthy, and climb my stairs at home. My leaves were blooming, my grass was greening, and winter was finally in my rear view. It was during this period where I was able to eventually carry the wheelchair that once carried me, and collapse the walker that once held me up. I was then discharged from home healthcare and completed my physical therapy at an outpatient rehabilitation site. Shortly thereafter, In February 2014, I was able to drive again! I began to thrive again! I could clearly see manifested spring-like events all around me!

I have learned so many life lessons from my affliction. These things have forever changed my life, my family's life, as well as those who experienced it with me. I've experienced the fall, winter, and spring. Now, I am extremely grateful to be able to write from a season of reflection, a season to be significant, a season of reward, and a season of graduation from the University of Wisdom....the Summer. Different from my summary written for the previous three seasons, I have decided to describe this season through the life lessons written in the following sections. It is my prayer that by the end of this book, you will have taken in the life lessons humbly submitted by me as well as the biblical application I used to assist me in presenting these lessons. Perhaps you will then be able to boldly share in my declaration that "It is GOOD that I was afflicted!" Enjoy!

SUMMER
Crutches

A crutch is a device that aids in the mobility of one who has been disabled. There are many types of crutches that have been created for many different reasons, but ultimately all for similar purposes…to offer TEMPORARY aid and support for one who has been temporarily disabled physically.

While hospitalized for three months, I was in a specially-designed hospital bed that offered ease to my painful surgical wound. You see, I was on a ventilator for a period of time, and because ventilators suck oxygen from your muscles, I experienced muscle atrophy (severe weakening of muscles and fiber due to physical inactivity). This was one of the contributing factors leading to the loss of my ability to walk. I wasn't able to begin physical therapy right away due to my wound, so my lower and upper body became very weak. Because of this current condition, I had to be cared for by other people. I had to wear a catheter to empty my bladder. When my rectum balloon could not properly hold my waste, nurses and technicians would have to turn me, discard my waste, and clean my backside. When it was time to eat my meals, others would have to pick up the phone and order my meals from the hospital cafeteria because I was too weak to hold the phone. When I would eat, others had to assist me in holding my utensils. When it was time to bathe, others would have to wash me. This was very humiliating to me because these are all things I'd been used to doing independently for most of my life! Being a man of pride and dignity, I struggled with needing others to do these things for me while having to just lay there. However, at some point, I had to allow others to help me…that is, if I didn't want to be a complete mess!

The reason why I disclosed the previous to you is because, although I was very uncomfortable needing outside assistance to perform simple tasks, I came to grips that these "crutches" were necessary for me to use! Having said that, over time I began to grow a little too accustomed to the crutch of the hospital bed along with the services and assistance of others doing things for me. I began to EXPECT the assistance at my beaconing call. The uncomfortable became very comfortable! I became so comfortable that, when it was time for me to start receiving physical therapy, I would tell them, "Just come back later. I need to rest!" That was nothing but laziness, procrastination, and comfort talking! That is until one day, my wife, "Drill Sargent" Tracy was there while the physical therapist came in, and just like every other day, I told them to come back. You see, I had become comfortable and relaxed in my current state because the crutches (nurses, caregivers, the specially-designed wound bed, etc..) offered me no challenge to doing something different! That particular day, once my wife saw that this resistance to physical therapy was becoming a norm for me, she slid her chair right up to my bedside and ever-so-softly said, "So, am I going to have to get used to rolling my husband around in a wheelchair for the rest of our lives, or DO YOU WANT TO WALK AGAIN? Honey, if you don't begin to use your limbs, you will lose your use of them! Now, Michael, LET THESE THERAPISTS HELP YOU GET YOUR STRENGTH BACK!" This little subtle pep talk from my wife hit me like a ton of bricks. It was JUST the wake-up call I needed to shift my mindset to embark upon the long journey of regaining my strength.

For many of you, it may not be a physical disablement that has caused you to use a crutch for "temporary support." It may be an emotional/spiritual crutch: a broken heart and finding yourself needing outside encouragement and validation. Perhaps you are in need of a financial crutch: maybe you currently need temporary government/public assistance due to some type of economical crisis beyond your control. This portion of the book was written just for you! If you currently find yourself in a life-altering situation that has caused you to depend on others for assistance (people and/or systems) as a crutch, I want you to remember these 3 things:

1. Embrace the "No Pain/No Gain" Principle….THERAPY HURTS!
2. You MUST set a goal and ACTIVELY-DELIBERATELY REACH FOR IT!
3. Crutches are only meant for TEMPORARY USAGE! Eventually, LOSE THE CRUTCH!

EMBRACE the "No Pain/No Gain" Principle…THERAPY HURTS!

Once I wrapped my mind around the fact that because I had not moved my legs and used my upper body for quite some time, physical therapy was going to be very uncomfortable and it was going to HURT! However, If I was going to regain strength, I would have to embrace the "no pain/no gain" principle. I became resolute in my mind that whatever the therapists asked me to do, whether it hurt or not, I was going to do it AND THEN SOME!

You Must Set A Goal and ACTIVELY-DELIBERATELY REACH FOR IT!

After several weeks of physical therapy, I finally gained enough strength in my core to sit up in the bed. Now, I had confidence for the next challenge. It was time for me to learn how to stand again. This proved to be a challenge within itself. I had to wear a gait belt to get assistance to stand. Regardless of that, right before the therapist would come to my room, I would imagine myself playing basketball again with my son, walking my daughter to the bus stop, and walking around freely while on vacation at Universal Studios…one of my favorite places! Make a mental note of this: in the process of recovering and getting better, YOU MUST HAVE IMAGES OF WHERE YOU WANT TO GO! You see, it's just like going on a long road trip. When my family goes on vacation to Orlando, Florida from Indianapolis, IN, it takes about 16 hours to get there by car. Many of my friends think that is too long of a road trip. I used to think the same thing, that is, until we realized the thousands of dollars we were saving by driving! Disney World, Universal Studios, the palm trees, and beaches is the destination we always look forward to enjoying. We knew that, no matter how long the journey would be, had we never completed mile number 1, we would never have reached mile number 970. You cannot get to Orlando, FL, the desired destination, if you never go through the pre-destinations or states that will eventually lead you to Orlando. Here's a nugget to remember: on the route to your desired destination, there are some locations and terrain along the way that YOU WILL NOT be able to avoid. You might as well go through until you get to! Jesus Christ Himself knew all about reaching His destination

(Hebrews 12:2 GWT),"Fixing our eyes on Jesus, the pioneer and perfecter of our faith. For the joy set before Him, He ENDURED His cross and DESPISED the shame (ignored the disgrace/embarrassment it brought Him)." Then He received the highest position in Heaven, the one right next to the throne of God. After wrapping our minds around the reality of the length of time it would take to get to Orlando, we began to LEARN HOW TO ENJOY THE JOURNEY! While you're reading this book and you are currently going through a physical, emotional, or financial setback, and you desire to regain strength and fortitude, I have some advice for you: though the journey may seem long, in order to arrive at your destination, KEEP YOUR FOOT ON THE GAS and KEEP DRIVING FORWARD only looking at the rear view mirror for reflection and not dwelling. Only stop to fill-up, rest, refresh and then get back behind the wheel and KEEP DRIVING!

Oftentimes in life, people fail to accomplish their goals due to a lack of planning to achieve those goals. Have you ever found yourself in this place? Do you know anyone like this? They want the most out of life, but plan the least. During this long and grueling rehab process, I have developed an entirely new appreciation for hard work. You see, before I became sick, it was very easy for me to know what I wanted in business and go hard after it with very routine planning and strategizing. However, having to learn how to walk all over again and everything that this milestone would require physically, emotionally, and spiritually, I had to set proper parameters. I had to learn how to celebrate bite-size victories and learn how to POLICE THE INTIMIDATION OF THE PROCESS! As I am writing this book, I am still re-learning how to properly balance myself and how to stabilize my walk while taking each step. I still have to plan each step I take so that I will not fall and injure myself. I'm still working hard every day to get back to walking normal. It's ok though! As long as I follow my plan (proper nutrition, working out, stretching, optimism, etc...), I WILL ACHIEVE MY GOALS! Listen to me, if you are going to achieve your goals and "walk again," slothfulness, laziness, and shortcuts MUST be removed from the table of options. Do you want to "walk again?" Then PLAN to walk and work hard and diligently at it! Proverbs 13:4 NLT states, "Lazy people want much but achieve little (lack of planning), but those who WORK HARD will prosper and will be richly supplied!" I challenge myself daily with this powerful proverb and I want to challenge you also. What area in your life has disabled you and your desire is to "walk again" or regain strength? Have you experienced "atrophy" (severe loss of strength) in your marriage, your finances, your education, your spiritual well being? Do you desire something different? Do you want better? If your answer is yes, I encourage you to set goals, first within your grasp, and secondly, just outside of your grasp. Follow through on your goals, celebrate bite-size victories along the way, and POLICE THE INTIMIDATION OF THE PROCESS! We're in this together!

Crutches are Only Meant for Temporary Usage.....Eventually LOSE THE CRUTCHES

If you haven't noticed by now, one of my main objectives in sharing my story is to parallel my physical experiences with wise spiritual and emotional life application. I am a firm believer that every God-allowed story is laced with nutrients that are very palatable for our physical, spiritual, and emotional well-being, and the level in which we are able to absorb these nutrients will directly affect our well-being as it relates to those 3 realms of our lives.

Such is the case with my advice and objective for the last point in this section: Crutches are Only Meant for Temporary Usage….Eventually LOSE THE CRUTCHES! If you have any plans to ever "walk again," you need to realize that DELIVERANCE IS PARTICIPATORY! In other words, NO ONE IS GOING TO DO IT FOR YOU! Can you imagine an arena full of screaming fans, cheerleaders, teammates, and coaches rooting for the best player on the team? It's the 4th quarter. The opposing team is up by 2 points with only 1.3 seconds remaining in the game. Everyone in the arena knows who's going to get the ball…the best player on the team! After all, that is when the best player normally performs at their best…under pressure! The coach has drawn up the best play to run in this clutch situation. The team is down by 2 points and the last time out has been taken and now it's time to execute the designed play. The crowd is screaming and cheering. Everyone is on the edge of their seat. Everyone is depending on the best player on the team to perform and make the clutch game-winning shot. The ball is inbounded into play. Each teammate rotates to their spot and now the ball gets passed to YOU KNOW WHO! There's only one problem! When the ball was passed to the star player….the best player…the clutch player,...the pass was intercepted by the opposing team and time ran out! What happened to the star player? Where was he when the ball was passed to him and everyone was depending on him to take the shot? Well, he got caught up and distracted by the crowds' cheers and praises. He never got into the right position after hearing CLEAR instructions from the coach during the final timeout! Can I tell you that YOU are the star player in the arena of your own life? Did you know that someone is watching and perhaps even depending on you to be in position so that you can properly execute the drawn up, God-designed play in order to get the victory…..even when opposing factors seem to be winning? When you CHOOSE to lose, others share in your defeat. However, when you CHOOSE to win, others get to share in your victory! You see, true champions learn how to play through injuries. What am I implying? Victory is not just your right, it is more less your choice and deliverance is participatory! The following are 3 scriptural references I would like to use in order to further inject my perspective on ridding yourself of the over-usage of your crutches:

First, let's take a look at one of Jesus' miracles recorded in John 5:5-9 ESV. (vs.5) There was a man who had been sick for 38 years. (vs.6) Jesus saw the man lying there and knew he had been laying there for a very long time. He asked the man, "DO YOU WANT TO BE MADE WELL (or healed)?" (vs.7) The man replied, "Sir, I have nobody to PUT ME IN the pool….and when I try to go, someone gets in my way!" (vs.8) To which Jesus replied, "GET UP! PICK UP YOUR MAT! WALK!" This was an interesting miracle by reason of its denotation of how a miracle is defined. A miracle is (1) an effect or extraordinary event in the physical world that surpasses all human or natural powers and is ascribed to a supernatural cause. (2) an effect or event manifesting or considered a WORK OF GOD. Long definitions, huh? The reason I mentioned that these definitions are interesting is because of the nature in which we have come to learn and define "a miracle." You see, oftentimes, when we sing songs like "I'm looking for a miracle, expecting the impossible,"……so on and so forth, in essence we're really saying that "I'm waiting around for something supernatural or out-of-this-world type of power to come and change my situation from worse to better because I'VE DONE ALL THAT I CAN DO!" Have you ever said this? Now, please don't get bent out of shape on me! I'll be the first one to declare that I whole-heartedly believe in the miracle-working power of Jesus Christ! He IS the one who delivered me from the jaws of death, for which I am eternally grateful! Having stated the previous, I still had work to do! You see, a miracle is an event that occurs when there are no further options that you can implement. This is when the MIRACLE WORKER goes to work! Someone has quoted before that "man's extremities is God's opportunity!" When you have actually come to the very end of yourself, that is when supernatural overrides begin to undergird (support) you! The work that I had to do and still have to continue to do is physical therapy. You see, internally, my organs were supernaturally restored (an extremity I could not fix on my own), however, if I was to ever gain strength to walk again and restore balance, it was going to require my participation. I'll rescue my point: DELIVERANCE OFTENTIMES REQUIRES YOUR PARTICIPATION! In the scripture, this man made a choice to believe that he could not get in the water though he was in the vicinity of the water. 38 years is a very long time.....enough time to convince ANYONE to merely settle into their current situation due to surrounding and contradictory circumstances. I'd like to call this mindset "complacency." This mindset causes one to find a permanent dwelling place in a situation that was only meant to be temporary and a bridge to greater things! This mindset sounds like this…"well, food stamps and unemployment checks AT LEAST keep me fed and a roof over my head," or " mama and grandmamma struggled to pay bills and robbed Peter to pay Paul, so this must be the way to do things!" Allow me to challenge you with this question: Do you want different? Do you want to be made well? If the answer is yes, are you willing to eliminate excuses, and change your mindset (John 5:7), are you willing to stop just hanging around your pool and get up and do something about your situation? You just might discover by doing so, just like this impotent man, he didn't even need to take a splash in the pool! He heard a word from the Lord, and just like the word he received from the Lord, I empower you with that same word

…GET UP, PICK UP YOUR MAT, and WALK! Jesus ignored this man's excuse and instructed him to activate what had always been inside of him…..something he could have done 38 years ago! I'm so grateful that we have a loving Heavenly Father who sees our potential beyond our pitiful excuses and continues to challenge us to activate what's always been inside of us in order to eventually accomplish goals and tasks; no matter how challenging.

Another example in scripture that clarifies my perspective on participatory deliverance is found in John 9. This story is about a blind man who was healed by Jesus. In verse 6 of this chapter, Jesus used unconventional methods to heal this blind man. Jesus used spit and dirt to make a paste, then anointed the eyes of this blind man. *Just a side note of acknowledgement: Jesus Christ, "the anointed one, the creator, and the very WORD OF GOD, had no earthly or logical reason for using saliva and dirt to make a healing balm for this affliction. After all, He created saliva and dirt! He is so sovereign that he can use WHATEVER material or method he chooses to and then call it anointing! This just lets me know that just in case I don't have a bottle of "blessed oil" or "anointing oil" on me (none of which I had on my person during ER, Operating Room, or, ICU), It is SO GOOD and REFRESHING to know that HIS healing anointing is not confined to the chemical properties of symbolic oil. Because he went to Gethsemane (the place of crushing) and then was crushed on the cross for MY healing and deliverance and YOUR healing and deliverance, it produced an everlasting oil and anointing that will forever cover me and destroy EVERY yoke!*

Ok, I'm back! In verse 7, Jesus gave this man instructions and without question, or consideration of the spit from another man's mouth, this blind man followed Jesus' instructions. He went, he washed at the pool instructed, and came back seeing! In verse 10, people asked him how he began to see and his reply was (vs 11), "A man called Jesus anointed my eyes with paste (or clay) and told me to go and wash my eyes. So I WENT, I WASHED, and I RECEIVED MY SIGHT!" So what is the point of this particular story of healing? Well, one point is that YOUR DELIVERANCE MAY BE CONTINGENT UPON YOUR WILLINGNESS TO PARTICIPATE IN AN UNCOMMON ACTIVITY! For instance, you may have been out of school for decades. You now have a family to support and bills to maintain, but you know that in order to improve your level of living and make more money, you need to go back to school and obtain more credentials and a higher skill set. Another instance; your marriage has become very routine and mundane. You started out with a burning flame of passion, romance, and consideration for her. Now it seems as if the flame is merely a spark at best. Perhaps instead of always just "bringing home the bacon" and having her to cook it; break the routine by making reservations and taking her on a night on the town. Send her a written invitation to a "night of her life" or even out of town on a second honeymoon! Intently listen to her every word. Let her know that you haven't forgot how wonderful she is and how enriched your life is by having the honor of her being in your life! (this can go both ways, ladies☺) All I am implying is that, if you desire to "see again," you have to be willing to "wash out" or eliminate whatever is causing you not to see a better life! What's amazing to me is that this blind man had more vision to see where he was headed than those who had 20/20 vision! Always be willing to abandon your routine and do things that you normally wouldn't do in order to obtain what you've never had or have been without for so long. The joy that comes with "abandoning the mundane to achieve much" cannot be explained! As I continue to work to regain strength and other physical abilities, I've learned to actively apply these principles daily. Again I say, WE'RE IN THIS TOGETHER!

My third clarification is derived from 2 Kings the 5th chapter. There was a man named Naaman who was a highly-decorated and respected commander of the Syrian army. However, in spite of his huge victories, his high regard from the king, his many trophies and triumphs, Naaman had a condition called leprosy. This was his issue/affliction. Regardless of all of his many accomplishments and awards, if Naaman didn't have the luxury of his armor to hide his leprosy, he would have been dishonorably discharged not only from the Syrian Army, but discharged from society as well! You see, leprosy was a disease that was so feared and frowned upon, that once a person was known to have it, they would be considered a social outcast. Naaman was a man of much pride and dignity, however, amongst his well-earned pride and dignity, dwelt two roommates called "arrogance and entitlement!"

Different than the two previous stories, I'd like to insert my points upfront. ARROGANCE and ENTITLEMENT WILL PARALYZE YOUR PARTICIPATION IN YOUR OWN DELIVERANCE CAUSING YOU TO HAVE LIMITED OR NO RESULTS! Similar to the previous story of the blind man, this story also involves unconventional methods. Naaman, a man of means and high influence, reminds me so much of a few fellow patients who were in the rehab hospital while I was there. Various ones came from very prominent backgrounds. Some were extremely wealthy businessmen, some were college professors, and then there were those in whom we would consider regular-old-joes. The fact of the matter was that, regardless of whatever pedigree or realm of social influence some of those people came from, in the rehab hospital, all inequalities were erased! We ALL had various afflictions and were in need of HELP! When you get admitted to the rehab floor, this is where cute-little leg stretches and massages cease and advanced physical therapy begins! This is the place where you will endure 3+ hours of daily therapy. This is the place where you get re-trained on how to live life independently. Nobody gives you anything! There are no reprieves! You are here to work hard, get strengthened, and not pampered! This is where you will be instructed to do things that you may feel are beneath you. Such was the case with many of these well-to-do patients. They thought that their arrogance and social influence they carried in the outside world was supposed to transfer into this environment. They expected breakfast to be brought to their bedside. They expected to be pampered around the clock with deluxe sponge baths. They thought that any and all available staff should cater to their every beckoning call. Even during physical therapy sessions, I watched many of them refuse to even try the various exercises that the therapists would instruct them to do. Though comical at times, it was sad to know that, if they continued to refuse to follow instructions from the experts, they would never recover and some would grow even worse!

As we examine Naaman's plight, we soon will discover that his arrogance and sense of entitlement almost kept him from participating in his own deliverance. Taking the liberty to use my imagination, Naaman (vs. 9) put on his designer tailor-made 3-piece suit, his expensive watch, his starched white shirt with embroidered initials on his cuffs, with his gold cuff links and alligator shoes, shined up his luxury sedan, and headed down (with his driver, of course) to the Prophet Elisha's house. Once he arrived to Elisha's house, his driver opened his door and Naaman got out of his car and stood at Elisha's door step; waiting and expecting to meet with the prophet. Much to Naaman's surprise, Elisha didn't even greet him nor did he come out to shake Naaman's hand! After all, Naaman was "the man" in his normal environment. In his position, he probably was used to people just anticipating the chance to meet the Syrian King's right-hand man. None of that stuff impressed Elisha. Just like the wealthy folks in the rehab hospital, those trained physical therapists and nurses couldn't care less about any of that! (vs 10) Elisha sent a message out to Naaman with instructions for him to follow in order to get deliverance from his leprosy. "Go wash in the 'muddy' Jordan River seven times and your leprosy will be cleansed," proclaimed the messenger to Naaman.

ARROGANCE

Could you imagine the look on Naaman's face? After all, he was already feeling disrespected by Elisha not coming out to greet him and now, "you want me to do WHAT!," Naaman probably thought. He wanted deliverance, but he wanted it on his own royal terms. How many times can you recall needing a serious change in your life but weren't receptive to the instructions required to be followed in order to bring forth those changes? Naaman rebuttled and said, "Dude, I'm dressed to impress! I'm suited and booted! Now your master Elisha not only wants me to get wet, but he wants me to get into the muddy Jordan too? I know Damascus has 2 very clean rivers that are cleaner than all the rivers in Israel! I'm out!" The verse actually states that Naaman "went off in a rage."

*FOLLOWING PROPER INSTRUCTIONS WILL ENSURE
DELIVERANCE!*

As previously mentioned, there were those in the rehab hospital who
refused to follow through on the instructions given by the therapists
due to their pride, arrogance, and sense of entitlement. They wanted
deliverance on their own royal terms! They preferred to "wash in the
2 Damascus Rivers" which represents the high society rather than
the "muddy Jordan River" which represented the regular-old-joes!
Many of you around the world that are reading this book have been
taking dips in the pristine waters of the Damascus River. You've
become so accustomed to doing things your way to the point to
where you can't see any other possibility working. Let me ask,
how's that been working out for you? Would you be honest enough
to admit that perhaps, due to your pre-injury status in life,
(prominence, wealth, accolades, etc…) it has caused a sense of
entitlement or maybe even a little pride to the point of being
unwilling to follow through on what it takes to rid yourself of your
"leprosy?" Naaman eventually was convinced to get past his
arrogant nature and participate in the instructions he was given and
he received his deliverance from his leprosy!

My dear readers, I am a firm believer that my situation was allowed
by God. He wanted me to re-enroll in the University of Wisdom in
order that I may be qualified to teach others how to properly
matriculate through the same university! You see, our majors differ,
but at the end, every one of our degrees will read the same; "this
student has completed the necessary courses and requirements for
the fulfillment of this degree!"

My affliction did not disable me. It has enabled me to be a greater
witness on behalf of Christ insomuch as to encourage those of you
who are currently going through to realize that CHAMPIONS ARE
THOSE WHO LEARN HOW TO PLAY THROUGH INJURIES!
For those life lessons and the opportunity to share them with you, I
can undoubtedly proclaim that, "IT IS GOOD THAT I WAS
AFFLICTED!"

SUMMER
Growing Better….Not Bitter!

Affliction is a God-accredited University of Wisdom with courses that vary in degrees of difficulty. The truth is that all of us will, at some point, be an alumni of this university; oftentimes with continuing education courses required. Those who graduate with honors are those who have decided to embrace the challenges of their assigned courses, learn from its lessons, and become BETTER. Those who belly-ache, complain, and refuse to learn, are those who fail the tests of their courses and find themselves in need of constant remediation. Those are the ones who decide to become BITTER. To those of you who find yourselves in the bitter portion of the class, You WILL NOT successfully complete your required course neither will you graduate until you embrace the challenges presented to you!

In Romans 8:18 (NLT), the Apostle Paul states, "Yet, what we suffer now is NOTHING compared to the glory He will reveal to us later." Now, let's employ a bit of etymology within this particular passage. In this scripture, Paul chose 2 distinct words to describe the optimistic nature of the "better" student as opposed to the pessimistic nature of the "bitter" student…….SUFFERING vs. GLORY. Suffering in the dictionary is defined as "the state of undergoing pain, distress, or hardship." Glory is defined as "high renown or honor won by notable achievements; magnificence; great beauty."

The perspective of the "bitter" student vs. the "better" student is clearly revealed within this scripture. You see, the bitter student only allows his/herself to see suffering. They are so inundated with the pain, distress, and hardship that they stop to over-analyze everything and conclude that the course is too heavy of a load. Consequently, they think about everything and never complete anything! However, the better student actually properly reads the syllabus and instructions of their course (the scriptures) and they discover something in this passage that, had the bitter student just read a little further, perhaps they would've become a better student. They would've discovered that by reading one more phrase past "suffer" was the word "NOW" (Reference Romans 8:18 NLT). This suggests that the phrase "suffering of this present time" offers hope that suffering is only TEMPORAL! When the better student read further instructions, they learned that the cause of undergoing temporary pain, affliction, hardship, and distress would produce an effect of high renown, honor won by notable achievements; magnificence; great beauty!

Me, being the "better" student that I am☺, I absolutely love the way Peter penned this perspective in 1 Peter 5:10 (NLT), "After you have suffered for a while (after embracing life's challenging courses), God HIMSELF will make you perfect. He will keep you in the right way. He will give you strength. He is the God of all loving favor and has called you through Christ Jesus to share His shining-greatness FOREVER!" Friends, when we go through our afflictions and learn the designed purpose for them, God, the president Himself, will come to you and personally reveal the greatness that always follows the grim. If you have allowed your heart to grow bitter and it has caused you not to pass the course, I want to encourage you that it is not too late to change your current mindset from bitter to better. Just pick up the instructions and read them completely. Realistically, a change in mindset will not necessarily happen overnight. After all, you didn't develop your current mindset overnight! However, if you are willing to "stay enrolled," continue to follow the instructions and the syllabus, then change will eventually occur. Friends, consider me your class orientation facilitator. I'd like to share a brief note of encouragement with you straight from the desk of the "President." This message has been recorded in your text book in the 16th chapter of the book of St. John (vs. 33), "I have told you about these sufferings so that IN ME you will have peace (calmness and serenity before, during, and after going through). In this world (while enrolled in this University of Wisdom), you WILL have trials and affliction, but be of GOOD CHEER! I HAVE OVERCOME THE WORLD! In other words, once you realize that there is a plan and a purpose for each and every affliction in your life, it will enable you to eliminate your bitterness and embrace your betterment! However, I believe that in order to really live a life of "better," we need to investigate the cause and root of your bitterness.

WHAT IS BITTERNESS?

Bitterness is a root: an underlying problem that does not always manifest on the outside, but rather in one's system.

By now, if you have been reading this book, you have realized that every lesson that I've been taught through my physical affliction has extracted spiritual principles from God's Word. This has empowered me to live through one of the most devastating experiences of my life! Having said that, let us explore more helpful tools and principles in God's Word regarding this opponent called bitterness. In the book of Hebrews 12:5 (NIV), the writer makes this suggestion, "See to it that none of you misses the grace of God and that no ROOT OF BITTERNESS springs up and troubles you. Many have been defiled (spoiled or impaired) by this root of bitterness."

"ROOT OF BITTERNESS SPRINGING UP"

A root is an unseen feeding source; a bubbling fountain of nutrients lying underneath the surface and are NEVER SEEN above the ground. It is a non-visible source of feeding for things which can be very publicly seen! In other words, that bad attitude, that snappy demeanor, or rudeness that others witness ON YOU is a manifested product of what is IN YOU! It is the harvested crop of a root system that has been planted in the underground of your very being. Mismanaged issues of life (hurt, harm, and disappointment) have festered and what others visibly witness is a representation of that invisible root of bitterness that has grown from a plant to a tree! There are many things that spring up from a bitter root system. See if you can find yourself in any of the following:

-Anger (easily upset over things)

-Negative Emotions Against others

-"I blame everyone else for everything without owning up to anything"

-Retaliation: A burning desire to "get even"

So, did you locate yourself in any of those examples? One of the biggest bitter-harboring attributes is retaliation. If you were to be honest, when something seemingly unmerited or undeserved occurs in our lives, such as financial windfall, sickness, relationship problems, etc…, isn't it true that many times we want someone to pay for it? Oftentimes, others get caught in the line of fire and become casualties of our anger and our relentless pursuit for revenge. How many times have you seen the news and an enraged husband, due to harboring years of anger towards his wife, decides to kill his wife and children? How many school shootings have occurred where one student became fed up with being bullied and disrespected by ONE of his peers, and then comes to school and takes multiple innocent lives in pursuit of retaliation towards ONE bully? How many times have you seen bosses (maybe your boss or maybe you are the boss) come to a pleasant work environment, but because they got chewed out by their superiors, they feel as if they need to dish some of that out to the employees underneath them? Here's one that breaks my heart;" MEN OF THE CLOTH." That's right! How many times have you been a part of the congregation at church and the sermon that the pastor is preaching is laced with bitterness and disguised as "revelatory impartation?" The sermon is laced with resentment and anger towards one or a few parishioners, but EVERYBODY has to listen to him/her randomly rant and rave. Listen, from one pastor to another, allow me to say this to my peers; Jesus (THE SHEPHERD) gave us (the under-shepherd) VERY CLEAR instructions to "feed my lambs," "tend to my sheep," and "feed my sheep!" He never instructed us to "shake my lambs," "beat my sheep," nor to "starve my sheep!" Pastors and spirituals leaders, we are to be the direct messenger and watchmen over HIS sheep. STOP GUNNING after the entire flock just to hit a few sheep! FEED them clear scripture….not scraps! Give them concepts…not crap! Breathe into them principles, precepts, and promises….not pollution! Put a swift end to your retaliation and render purposeful revelation…not random rantings! We are supposed to be vanguards. That is, a group of people leading the way and helping to advance those who we have been entrusted to lead. Bitterness will cause our ministries to digress rather than progress. NONE OF US win unless/until we do it Christ's way and for His glory alone!

Although the previous was intentionally directed towards my peers, you can also apply this to your lives as well. You see, bitterness can prevent you from realizing the very purpose of why you had to experience your affliction. You will not be able to declare with sincerity that, "IT IS GOOD THAT I WAS AFFLICTED!"

TOP GRADUATE OF AFFLICTION

The following biblical character was one who, after she got past her bitterness, was able to realize the next principle I learned: THERE IS PURPOSE IN YOUR AFFLICTION!

Allow me to preface this awesome story by reiterating that, regardless of your affliction, famine, or situation in life, NONE OF IT CATCHES GOD BY SURPRISE! In the words of my daughter, "God never says OOPS!" While we are often caught off guard by a crisis, He is never in crisis-mode. Since such is the case, our next move and focus should be to investigate what God's design and purpose is for choosing us to experience what we experience. King Solomon, the wisest man to have ever lived on this earth, confirms my principle of realizing that every situation we experience has a direct connection to the sovereignty of God (Ecclesiastes 3:1 NIV), "To EVERYTHING there is a SEASON, and a time to EVERY PURPOSE under the heaven." This is part of the class syllabus and a stark requirement for graduating from the University of Wisdom! Let's investigate PURPOSE in the following case study found in the book of Ruth.

When studying this short-but-powerful book, the title character (Ruth) often gets most of the attention. However, there are oftentimes even more powerful lessons we can learn from the supporting cast…particularly a woman by the name of Naomi. Her story begins in the city of Bethlehem, meaning the "House of Bread." A famine hits Bethlehem and Naomi's family moves to another place. However, Naomi leaves "full" (or complete) because she still has her husband, Elimilech, and her two sons, and they are all headed to a place not affected by the famine….a place called the "Fields of Moab." In Moab, her sons marry, but before this happens, Naomi's husband dies. Some time later, both of her sons die also.

This is where Naomi's pain and tragedy begins; the pain and devastation of loss of the greatest magnitude.

Within a very short period of time, Naomi experiences some of the most shattering losses in the human experience; the loss of a spouse and two children. It would be bad enough to lose a spouse, and even worse to also lose perhaps one child, but two children? And both children were boys? You see, in times of old, it was a mark of high social and economic status to have a son. It would be equivalent to one having retirement wealth or generational wealth. A male child would be able to carry on the family's name in the event of the father's death. This is why the bible says that Naomi was "full." Can you imagine how empty Naomi must feel right now? Could you imagine the stress of JUST burying your spouse and without a moment to completely grieve that loss, you have to find the emotional fortitude to bury your two sons? This woman was bereaved, broken, but most of all, she had grown bitter! She lost the three men in her life, thus losing her financial security. Have you been here before; where life was going great, the birds were chirping, the sun was shining bright, and then.....BOOM......out of seemingly nowhere the clouds begin to gather, the colorful beauty of the sun turned gray, and the chirping birds seemed to start pecking you? Can you imagine having your secure economic floor collapsing right from up under you WITHOUT ANY NOTICE?

Although the scripture's text doesn't go into further detail, there are some other factors that may have added to Naomi's bitterness. You see, when famine (loss and scarcity) came to Bethlehem (House of Bread), Elimilech, Naomi's late husband, decided to relocate his family to the fields of Moab. Without further investigation into the scriptures as it pertains to time and culture, one would nod in favor of Elimilech's decision to get his family away from a land of presumably limited supply. However, upon further review of the scripture, we find that Elimilech, from the Tribe of Judah (a people who always praise God), whose name means "God is my king and my source," was already a man of sufficient means. Even though Bethlehem was experiencing great famine, Elimilech's family was more than sufficient to handle the famine. So why, you might ask, would this man relocate his family to another place, especially a place like Moab? The truth is that Elimilech left Bethlehem so that beggars and those displaced by the famine wouldn't come to his door begging for things during the famine. This selfish mindset connected Elimilech with the very meaning of Moab, "a land of misguided kindness or a land of false hospitality." Moab was the same nation that refused bread and water to the Israelites (God's chosen people) when they came up from Sinai. So, to add to Naomi's bitterness was the fact that, because they were already secure and famine-proof, there was no need for her husband to relocate them to a place that had no reverence for God nor any authentic hospitality! They left Bethlehem, a warm and friendly environment, to go to the fields of Moab, an open and unprotected place. Bible writings suggest that an empty field is an image that often precedes tragedy, and as we've learned, Naomi's husband's decision to leave Bethlehem would be followed with the pain of emptiness and loss.

To digress just a bit, before Naomi's sons died, they married two Moabite women. Their names were Orpah and Ruth. Not only was Naomi widowed, but her daughters-in-law were now widowed as well. When Naomi returned to Bethlehem, her daughters-in-law returned with her. They also lost their source of security. If I were to have the chance to interview Naomi at this point of her tragic plight, I would ask her what lessons or points of advice she would offer us having gone through these series of events so far.

ADVICE TO US FROM NAOMI:

1. "The grass is not always greener somewhere else. Moab may have seemed more plush and green, but that was just spray paint!"
2. "Just because God allowed famine to occur in your "place of bread" does not mean that there is no more bread or provision!"
3. "Remember, it's Bethlehem, Judah and though famine may hit your city (Bethlehem), you're still in a STATE OF PRAISE (Judah)! "

Thanks Naomi! Naomi had a lot of emotions to deal with. Even when she returned to Bethlehem, she urged her daughters-in-law to go back to their native land of Moab; not because she didn't love them, but because they were still young women and had a much better chance of remarrying and having more sons. You see, Naomi was an elderly woman, past the age of child bearing and with no husband and no sons to redeem the family's property, she presumably will lose the property as well. Bitterness even caused Naomi to be a bit sarcastic when she told Ruth and Orpah, "Even if I could remarry and have two more sons, what are you going to do….wait until they grow up and marry them?" She was so bitter that, when her friends greeted her upon returning to Bethlehem, she told them to "call me Mara, because the Almighty has made my life very bitter. I went away full but the Lord has brought me back empty. Why call me Naomi? The Lord has afflicted me; the Almighty has brought misfortune, disaster, and catastrophe on me!" Remember a few paragraphs ago, we noted that you know you are bitter when you begin to blame others for your plight in life. Naomi, in this instance, blamed God! Naomi's name means "pleasant and delightful," but her bitterness made her want to change her name. Understandably so because there is NOTHING on the surface that would suggest anything pleasant or delightful.

My dear readers, and fellow students of U.W. (University of Wisdom), the pain of affliction forced Naomi to want to change her very name from "pleasant and delightful" to Mara "bitter." I want you to take notice and be very dutiful to police the intimidation that will accompany your afflictions. Don't allow the pain to cause you to miss out on the purpose for which God allowed it to occur. Don't allow situations in life to change your identity from "pleasant and delightful" to "bitter!" I know how it feels to have your private pain to be put on public display. Pride will cause you to try and protect your true nature by wanting people to see you in a different way than what you were created to be. Therefore, you try to hide behind an emotional mask and oftentimes, it will give you instant comfort but you will soon find out that anything that has been altered from its original state will require lots of maintenance to upkeep! And no matter how long you have the ability to upkeep what you're not, eventually your upkeep will end up being your downfall! What am I saying to you? Simply this: even when you don't understand in totality why you've been selected to go through your affliction, stay true to who you were created to be! After all, God knows who you are and who he has created you to be. He has a perfect plan and purpose for your affliction!

As I told you earlier in this book when I wrote about the various seasons of my life during my experience, allow me to reassure you right now of God's words to me, "WHILE YOU'RE EXPERIENCING AN UNFAMILIAR ATMOSPHERE AND CAN'T SEE ME, I SEE YOU!" You may have gone from six figures, and at no fault of your own, you went to no figures. God says, "I SEE YOU!" You may have lost loved ones to seemingly untimely deaths. Be assured in knowing that GOD SEES YOU! Since we have this immutable truth, please rest in the assurance that God is using your affliction for His Glory….for your story! In Psalm 139:11-15 summarized David's intimate conversation with God, a conversation that any of us could have with Him. "Even darkness can't hide from you! Darkness and light are both alike to you! You had me covered even when I was in my mother's wound! I will praise you because I am fearfully and wonderfully made!" Dear reader and fellow students, don't have an identity crisis when problems arise, but instead, identify Christ in the midst of your crisis! The prophet Isaiah assures us in Isaiah 59:19 that it is not a matter of "if" but a matter of "when" as it pertains to on-coming afflictions. He wrote, "When the enemy comes in (or God allows him admission into your life) LIKE A FLOOD, the Spirit of the Lord will lift up a standard (a banner of victory) against him." You see, even the enemy is on God's payroll! So when he comes in acting or even looking LIKE A FLOOD, he is not doing anything without the hand of God's approval stamped on it! Remember, NOTHING SNEAKS UP ON GOD or CATCHES HIM BY SURPRISE! And because of that, you know that whatever you have to face while enrolled in this University of Wisdom, the end result is God's banner of victory on your behalf!!!

MORE ADVICE FROM NAOMI

"If the Lord has ever "brought you back empty" (allowed you to experience great heartache and pain), Trust me, HE IS UP TO SOMETHING! Stay pleasant and delightful! He does all things PERFECTLY! Trust his plan! "

Revelations 21:5 says, "He that sits on the throne said,'Behold (Look and see), I make all things new!" Isaiah 43:18-19 (NLT) encourages us to, "…forget all that old stuff! It is nothing compared to what I am going to do. For I am about to DO SOMETHING NEW. SEE I ALREADY BEGUN! DO YOU NOT SEE IT? I WILL MAKE A PATHWAY THROUGH THE WILDERNESS. I WILL CREATE RIVERS IN THE DRY WASTELAND (the desert; the place of loneliness, and abandonment)."

ANOTHER POINT OF ADVICE FROM NAOMI

"I learned that my loss/famine was a SEED that God wanted to use to propel me into my harvest! God is not as interested in your famine as He is in the purpose for your famine/seed which is YOUR HARVEST!" God says in Jeremiah 29:11,*" I know the plans I have for you, declares the Lord. They are plans for peace and not disaster, plans to give you a future filled with hope."*

God never allows LOSS in your life without GAIN being on His mind. Luke 18:28 (NLT), Peter told Jesus, "We've left our homes and worldly possessions to follow you. 'Yes', Jesus replied, 'and I ASSURE YOU that everyone who has given up house or wife or brothers or parents or children for the sake of the kingdom of God, will be REPAID MANY TIMES OVER IN THIS LIFE and will have ETERNAL LIFE in the world to come!" The thing(s) you have lost that seem to be irreplaceable to you, God has ALREADY designed a better replacement that's SEVEN TIMES GREATER than what you've lost! Ruth 4:14-16 confirms this fact. This was a statement recorded from events following Naomi's restoration and the end of her bitterness. I encourage you to read the complete story from the bible. The women of the town told Naomi in verse 15, "May he restore your youth and care for you in your old age. For he

is the son of your daughter-in-law who loves you and has been
BETTER TO YOU THAN SEVEN SONS!"

In closing, Naomi was able to overcome bitterness, maintain her
identity, and ultimately realize and fulfill the purpose for her
affliction. She was chosen to be a mentor for her young daughter-in-
law Ruth. Her ability to find the "better" beyond the "bitter" made
way for the biggest shift and comeback that she had ever
experienced in her life! As you previously discovered, her daughter-
in-law Ruth would prove to be "better than seven sons" to Naomi.
Her obedience to her God-given purpose made inroads for the most
important entrance of deliverance that we could ever ask for. You
see, Ruth married a wealthy man named Boaz who reserved the right
to REDEEM all that Ruth had lost by marrying her. This kinsman
redemption not only covered Ruth, but the wealth that Naomi lost
through her husband's death would be restored and redeemed as
well! Not only was her economical status restored, her social status
was also restored because Ruth had given Naomi a son to raise! How
awesome is that? God is THE ONLY ONE who has the power and
sovereignty to subtract in order to add! I often say that GOD IS
BACKWARDS, for He knows the end from the beginning. He's the
ONLY BEING that can press "rewind and forward" at the same
time, BECAUSE HE IS TIME and, as David said in Psalms 139:11-
15,"…..darkness and light are the same to you!" It would be
impossible for our God to wear sunglasses in order to shade the light
because he is NOTHING BUT LIGHT! He is "so much GOD" that
it's impossible for him to quench his own thirst because HE IS
WATER! And guess what? It is impossible for him to be enlightened
or learn something new because HE KNOWS EVERYTHING! He
already knew how you were going to come out of your affliction
before you even began to experience it! WHO IS LIKE THE
LORD? NOBODY! Boaz and Ruth had a son named Obed. Obed
was the father of Jesse. Jesse was the father of David, and we know
who came through David's lineage….Jesus Christ, the most
important entry into this world that we could ever have! Naomi's
many afflictions were purposeful so that the world could eventually
see Christ. Let me ask you; Could it be that you're so bitter about
your God-ordered affliction that it is literally causing someone in
your world to NOT see Christ? I am convinced that this is why I was

chosen to experience my affliction. I'm a man of pride and dignity, so when I was challenged by God to write this book, and was instructed to be very transparent and show my actual wounds, I asked God "why?" The answer was very clear. He answered, "Don't be ashamed to show your open wounds! I'm still showing mine and I want to use the wounds of your affliction as a guide to allow people to see my open wounds!"

Psalm 34:19 states that, "Many are the afflictions of the righteous, but the Lord delivers him out of them all!" My dear reader, your afflictions may be many and the end of it may not be in sight, but the previous scripture confirms another immutable truth….the Lord, in His own timing, will deliver you out of ALL of them! Knowing this is the end result, take my advice that, if you settle into the purpose of your situation, stay enrolled in class and don't drop out, you and others will be able to glean from your experiences and say with all truth and sincerity……

IT IS GOOD THAT I WAS AFFLICTED!!!

CLASS DISMISSED!

WARNING!

PLEASE BE ADVISED THAT THE FOLLOWING PAGES CONTAIN GRAPHIC IMAGES OF MY WOUND AND IMAGES OF MY HOSPITAL AND REHAB EXPERIENCES.

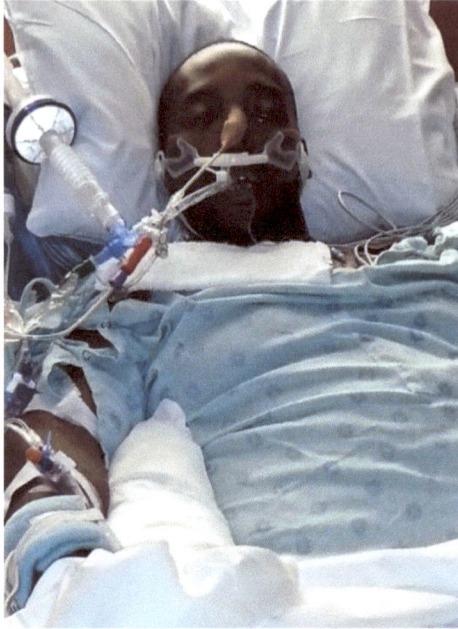

Image of me in ICU after 1st surgery
(Aug 5, 2013)

Image of me over a month after being released from ICU
(Sept 21, 2013)

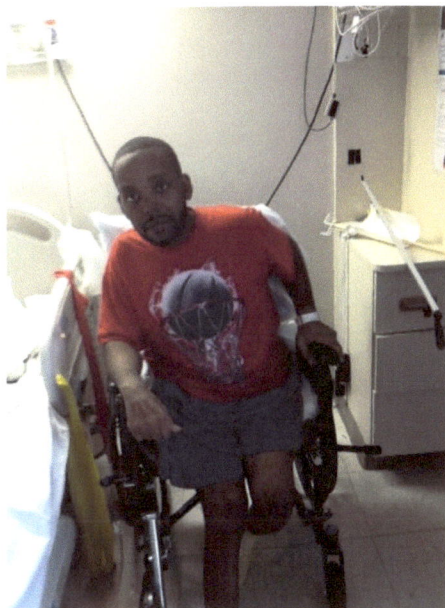

Image of me in rehab only weighing 106lbs
(Oct 2013)

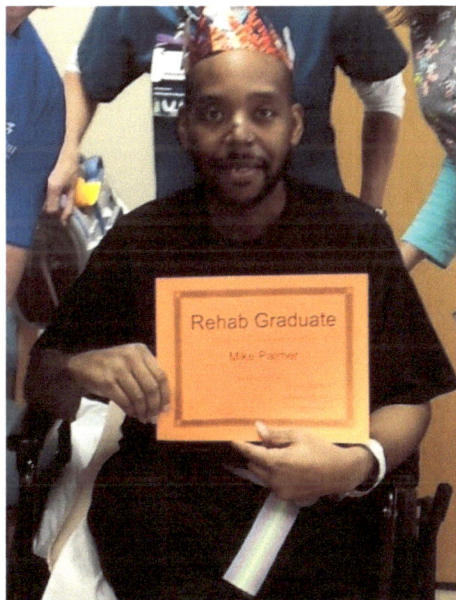

Graduating from rehab
(Oct 23, 2013)

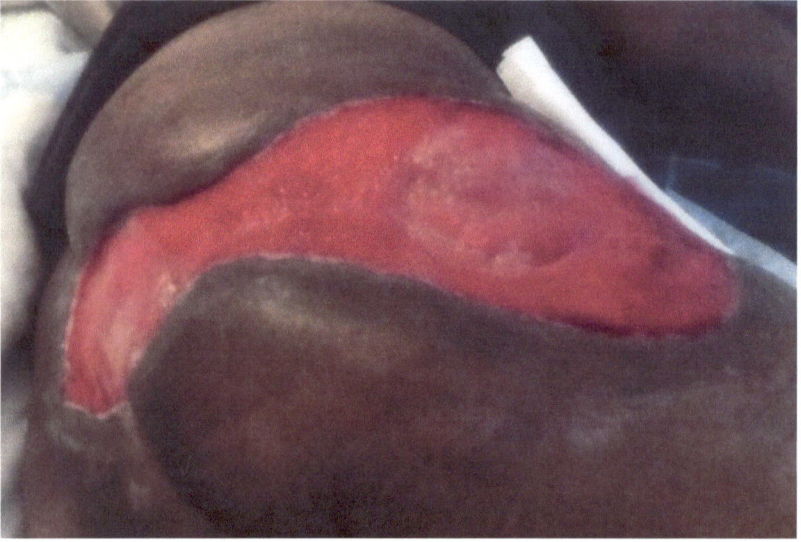

This is the first time a photo was taken of the wound during a wound change at home. By this time flesh had grown back in and it was in the healing process. In August 2013, the wound was much larger, only the hip bone was exposed, and none of the flesh you see here was visible.
(Nov 4, 2013)

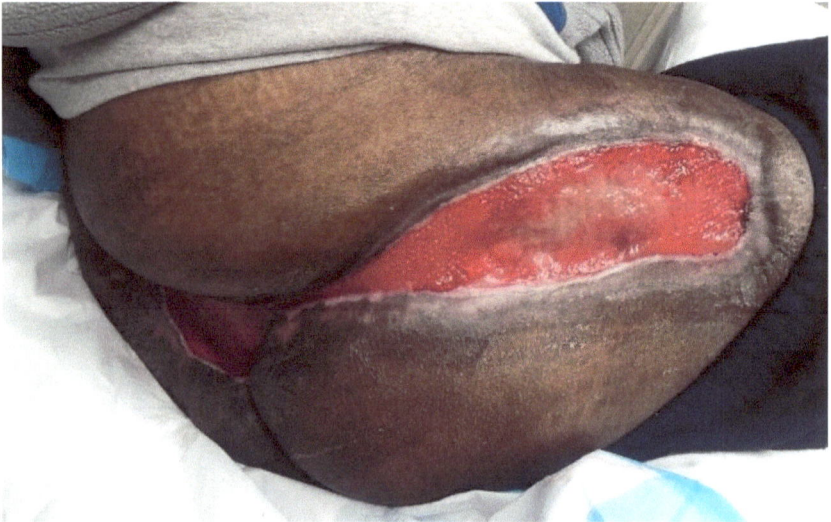

Image of wound before skin graft
(Dec 11, 2013)

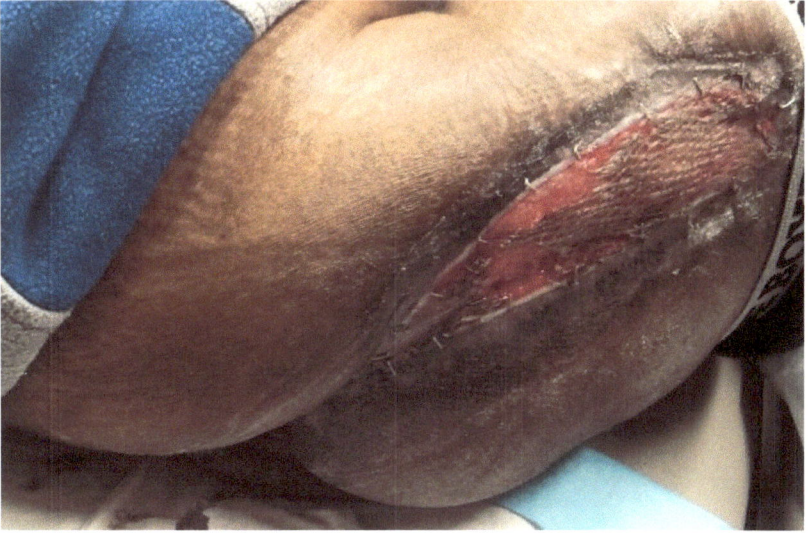

Image of wound after skin graft
(Dec 23, 2013)

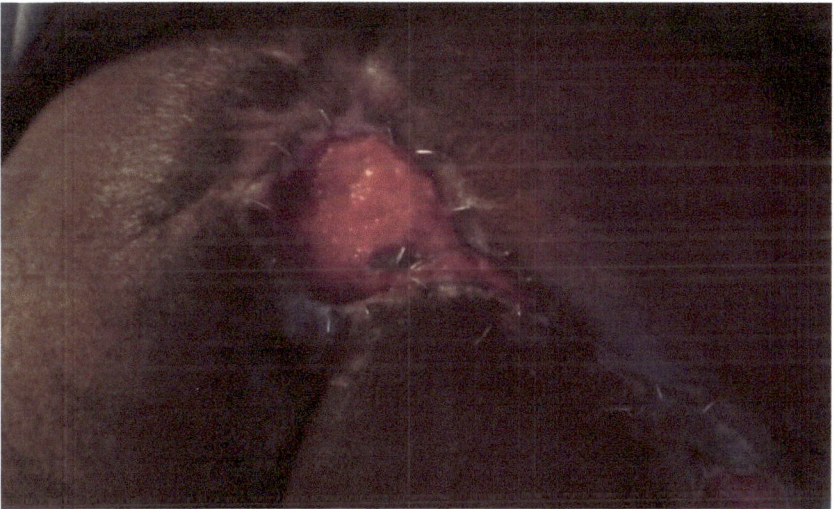

Image of healing progress of wound after skin graft
(Jan 4, 2014)

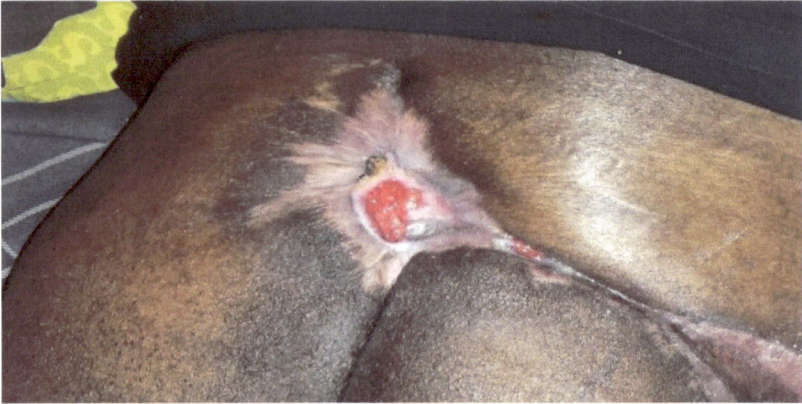

Image of wound almost two months after skin graft
(Feb 16, 2014)

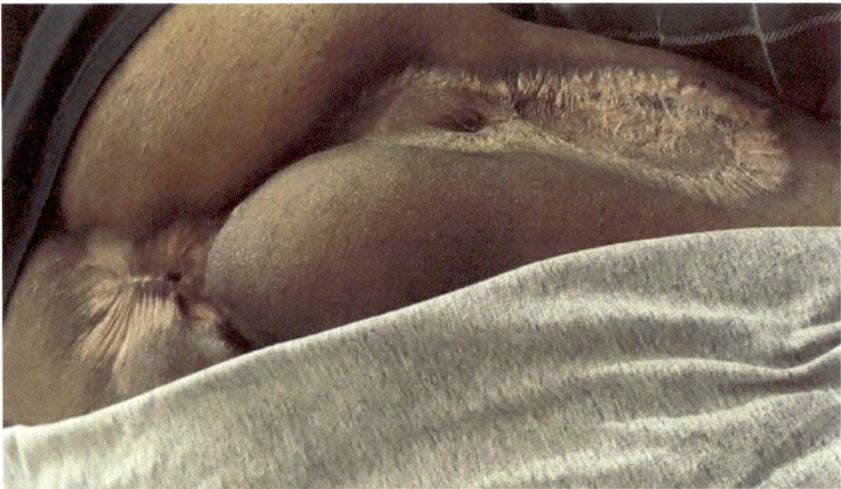

Final image of wound completely healed (now called a "shark bite")
(March 2016)

www.ingramcontent.com/pod-product-compliance
Lightning Source LLC
LaVergne TN
LVHW010027070426
835513LV00001B/2